STRENGTHS-BASED TEAMS

Why Leveraging Strengths Accelerate Business Results

For permission requests,
write to the author at the address below.
Leadership Alive, Inc. | PO Box 69652 | Tucson, AZ 85737

ISBN: 979-8-9886661-7-2 (paperback)
ISBN: 979-8-9887643-7-3 (hardback)
ISBN: 978-1-64316-185-3 (ebook)

LeadershipAlive.com

Printed in the United States of America
Author: Christopher P. Meade, PhD
Cover design by Kevin Piazza
Editing Team: Rob Peace & David Elmore

Contents

1.
Setting the Stage

Embracing our strengths is akin to unearthing priceless gems; they enrich our lives, illuminate our path, and make us truly invaluable.

Unearthing Hidden Gems

What if I told you that you possess a unique superpower? A set of attributes so personal, so potent, that they can propel you and your organization to dizzying heights of success. Sound like a fanciful science fiction plot? Perhaps, but it couldn't be more true. This is the promise of a strengths-based approach in business—and it's more science than fiction.

As you know, we live in an era of innovation, where companies constantly seek an edge to stay out front. Amid all the jargon and buzzwords about "getting ahead," one term has emerged from the fray, a word that captures attention like no other—strengths. It's not merely an old-school notion of muscle and might; it also refers to the intricate tapestry of talents, skills, knowledge, and raw potential that reside within each of us. These are the hidden gems that are waiting to be discovered, polished and integrated into your newly super-powered business engine.

Every superhero story starts with the discovery of a unique ability—the moment Peter Parker realizes he can climb walls, or Harry Potter discovers he's a wizard. Like these iconic characters, each of us carries within us a unique blend of talents and strengths. However, we often go through life—indeed our careers—unaware of our true potential. This is where the power of strengths plays out. So we must identify and cultivate our "superhero" gems.

But what exactly *is* a strength? In simple terms, it's something you're naturally good at and enjoy doing—an activity that energizes you, a task you get lost in. When you're leveraging your strengths, you're in your zone. Psychologists call it being "in flow."[1] But more than just a feel-good factor, using your strengths correlates strongly with increased productivity, higher levels of engagement, and overall job satisfaction. It's like a magic potion for high performance.

And it's not just confined to individuals. Teams and organizations gain immensely from adopting a strengths-based approach—creating a dynamic entity. It's like a band of superheroes, if you will, where each member brings their unique strengths to the table, creating a synergy that propels the team toward high performance and exceptional results.

Leadership, too, gets a mega boost from this approach. A strengths-based leader doesn't merely oversee their team—they empower it. They don't just command—they cultivate. These leaders act like talent alchemists, transforming potential into high performance. They become the gardeners who nurture the seeds of talent, enabling team members to bloom in their own unique way

At an organizational level, a strengths-based approach can trigger a revolution. These aren't mere workplaces but rather ecosystems that thrive on the power of strengths. The culture reverberates with the spirit of high performance, engagement, and job satisfaction. It's a potent catalyst for organizational success, delivering a punch in productivity, profitability, and positive work culture.

This book will be your guidebook on your incredible strengths jour-ney—taking you on an exploration of the strengths landscape and providing you with the tools to unearth your strengths, as well as guiding you in building strengths-based teams and organizations.

---

[1] The concept of "flow" was popularized by psychologist Mihaly Csikszentmihalyi in his 1990 book *Flow: The Psychology of Optimal Experience.*

You're absolutely ready to unearth your hidden gems, leverage your strengths, and trigger a revolution in your team and organization. Let's dive in and see how we can unravel the power of strengths, charting a formidable course toward business success.

Leadership and Management

OK, so let's unmask the superpower of strengths-based leadership and organizations. We'll start with an apt musical metaphor.

In an orchestra, each musician is a virtuoso, a master of their instrument. When they play alone, sure, they make beautiful music. But in concert with others, led by a maestro who understands their strengths and knows how to harmonize them, they create something extraordinary. They create a symphony. This is the essence of strengths-based leadership, creating a symphony of strengths that drives exceptional organizational performance and results.

In leadership, the strengths-based approach requires a radical shift from traditional command-and-control to empowerment and cultivation. Instead of focusing on weaknesses and trying to fix them, strengths-based leaders focus on strengths and aim to develop them. They manage weakness rather than fixate on it. This approach transforms leaders from being just bosses to being catalysts for growth, from taskmasters to talent alchemists. The magnetic pull of such leadership not only attracts talent but also nurtures and retains it, and it creates a potent talent pool that fuels the organization's success.

Such leaders understand the unique strengths of their team members and how they can be harmonized for maximum effect. This understanding enables them to delegate wisely, assigning roles that align with individual strengths, fostering a collaborative environment where everyone feels valued and engaged. This, in turn, leads to increased productivity, higher job satisfaction, and lower turnover rates—the hallmarks of a successful team and organization.

Strengths-based organizations recognize, revere and develop strengths. They've successfully built a strengths-based ecosystem, a place where every process, every interaction, and every decision is guided by the strengths philosophy. They have successfully inculcated a strengths-based culture that resonates with high performance, engagement, and satisfaction.

But what does this mean in concrete terms? What are the tangible benefits of becoming a strengths-based organization? Let's turn to some compelling evidence.

Gallup—A Trailblazer

Gallup, an American advisory and analytics company that's one of the leading proponents of the strengths-based approach, underscores the measurable benefits of a strengths-based approach to management and employee engagement. It boasts:

1. **Reduced turnover.** According to Gallup's 2020 report titled "Building a High-Development Culture Through Your Employee Engagement Strategy," teams who receive strengths-based development have up to 19% less turnover in historically high-turnover organizations.

2. **Increased customer engagement.** The same 2020 report found that work units receiving strengths feedback have 8.9% greater profitability and indicated that strengths-based organizations have higher customer engagement.

3. **Increased profit/productivity.** In a 2015 Gallup report, "Strengths-Based Employee Development: The Business Results," it found that a focus on strengths leads to a 10% to 19% increase in sales, a 14% to 29% increase in profit, and a 6% to 16% lower turnover rate.

4. **Engagement and performance.** In a 2014 Gallup study titled "How Employees' Strengths Make Your Company Stronger," it revealed that work units in the top quartile of engagement are 21% more productive and have 22% higher profitability than work units in the bottom quartile.

Sounds like the secret sauce to organizational success, right? But these statistics aren't just about improved business results—strengths-based organizations also excel in fostering a positive work culture. They become talent magnets, attracting and retaining the best in the industry. They foster a culture of learning and growth, creating places where everyone is encouraged to develop their strengths and reach full potential. These companies breed loyalty and commitment, establishing environments where employees aren't just satisfied but engaged and inspired.

But the case for strengths-based leadership and organizations doesn't end with these tangible benefits. The real beauty of this approach lies in its transformative power—the ability to change the way we view ourselves and others, the way we work, the way we lead, and, ultimately, the way we succeed.

The Symphony of Strengths

On our exciting journey, you'll discover the myriad ways in which a strengths-based approach revolutionizes your management style, your team, and your organization. You'll learn how to identify and develop your strengths and those of your team. You'll discover how to build a strengths-based team and organization, and how to navigate the accompanying challenges.

Strengths-based management isn't about *being* a superhero. It's about recognizing and unlocking the superheroes *within your team.* It's about understanding that your team isn't just a group of individuals but a dynamic blend of diverse strengths. It's about nurturing an environment where each team member capitalizes on their strengths, and weaknesses are minimized. And it's about fostering an environment of shared respect, where each person's strengths are acknowledged, appreciated, and utilized to achieve common goals.

Strengths-based organizations create a holistic ecosystem thriving on strengths—embedding the strengths philosophy into the DNA of the organization, and instilling strengths into every process, decision, and interaction. And it's about building a culture where everyone—from top leadership to frontline employee—understands their strengths, values the strengths of others, and knows how to leverage these for collective success.

Embracing a strengths-based approach at the leadership and organizational level can feel like a seismic shift. But the rewards are monumental when everyone feels valued and engaged. A strength-based focus creates a ripple effect where productivity soars and success isn't just about meeting targets but about continuous growth and development. Strengths-based leadership is primarily people-based, rather than results-based. Leaders aren't just managers but mentors. This is the power of strengths-based leadership in teams and organizations, and it's the potential that awaits you when you embrace the strengths revolution.

As we blast off into this strengths-based universe, you'll encounter numerous insights, strategies, and practical tools to help you on your journey. You'll learn the art and science of identifying strengths. You'll discover the intricacies of nurturing a strengths-based team and the strategies imperative to cultivating strengths-based leadership.

Yes, strengths-based leadership is about creating that symphony of strengths. It's about the maestro and the musicians, the leader and the team, the organization, and its people—all coming together in perfect harmony, each leveraging their own strengths to create a masterpiece that resonates with success.

As you make your way through these pages, you're not just reading; you're embarking on a journey—a strengths journey. One that promises to transform you as a manager, a team, and an organization. One that offers a compelling blend of personal growth, team development, and organizational success. It's a journey that's sure to make you stop, reflect, and beam, "Wow, I never knew we had this much potential!"

Let's unravel the magic of strengths together and explore the wonders of strengths-based teams, uncovering the power of strengths-based leadership. In doing so, we'll create a strengths-based revolution in our organizations. The journey to a brighter, strengths-based future begins *now*.

Team Discussion Questions

1. What unique strengths do you feel you bring to the team, and how have they contributed to collective successes so far?

2. Can you think of an example of when your unique strengths were leveraged for the benefit of the team? How did that influence the result?

3. As a team, how do we currently identify and nurture our individual strengths? Are there areas where we can improve?

4. How does our current leadership style foster or inhibit the development of individual strengths? How might we change this for the better?

5. How does our organization integrate a strengths-based philosophy into its culture? Are there ways we can further enhance this?

6. How can we better harmonize our individual strengths to create a more effective team "symphony"?

7. Reflecting on our team dynamics, can you think of a scenario where someone's strength wasn't utilized fully? How might we ensure that every team member's strength is being used to its maximum potential?

2.
Revealing the
Magic of Strengths

Strengths aren't just skills; they're the invisible wings
that let your talents soar. Identifying them is like
discovering you've been a superhero all along, and
understanding them is your journey to
master your superpowers.

Identifying and Understanding Your Superpowers

Superman can fly. Spiderman spins and slings webs. Iron Man—
well, he's a tech-savvy genius. And just like these fictionalized he-
roes, we've got a unique set of strengths—our very own superpowers. They're hiding in plain sight—like Clark Kent—waiting to be
discovered and unleashed.

But, of course, our superpowers don't come with a flashy cape or a
dramatic origin story. Instead, they're woven into the fabric of our
everyday lives, reflected in the things we naturally excel at and in
the activities that energize us. They might be as straightforward as
being an exceptional listener, or perhaps having an uncanny knack
for spotting patterns in data. Maybe it's being able to charm a room
full of people without breaking a sweat.

Now, you may be thinking, "Those don't sound much like superpowers to me." They are. Remember that "hiding in plain sight"
thing? The key to unlocking your personal superpowers lies in identification and understanding. We're not talking about a quick skim
through a list of generic skills. No, we're talking about a thought-
ful, intentional exploration of what makes you uniquely *you*. This

is where we break away from the cookie-cutter approach and focus on your distinct blend of strengths.

First up, there's self-reflection. This is where you take a time-out from the hustle and bustle, sit down with yourself, and ask, "What am I naturally good at? What activities make me lose track of time? When do I feel most like myself?" Think back to the moments when you've felt most successful and fulfilled. What were you doing? What skills were you using? These are your clues. They're the breadcrumbs leading you to your superpowers.

Next up is feedback. You turn to others—family, friends, colleagues, and mentors—those who know you well and have seen you in action. Talk to them. What strengths do they see in you? What do they feel you naturally excel at? Those who care about us can often spot our strengths even when we're oblivious to them— because we've taken them for granted. We wouldn't even describe them as strengths, but with their input, we can seem them anew.

Finally, there are strengths-assessment tools, such as Clifton-Strengths, StandOut, or VIA Character Strengths. These methods aren't the be-all and end-all, but they can provide valuable insights, especially when paired with self-reflection and feedback. They're based on extensive research and can help you to identify your top strengths.

As you can imagine, identifying your personal superpowers isn't a one-and-done thing. It's a journey, a process of continual discovery and understanding—an exploration worth embarking on. Because the more we understand our strengths, the more effectively we can use them. The more we use them, the more we grow. And the more we grow, the more we can contribute to our team and organization.

So, here's to unmasking our personal superpowers, to discovering the unique blend of strengths that make us who we are. Here's to transforming our everyday skills into extraordinary capabilities and shifting our potential into powerful performance. Here's to the magic of individual strengths!

Harnessing That Magic

Discovering the power of your strengths is like turning on a lighthouse in the fog. It guides your way, illuminates your path, and leads you to your best self. And when you're operating from your best self, you're in your element, achieving more than you ever thought possible.

During this discovery and practice, you'll notice a shift in your mindset—viewing challenges as opportunities to flex your superpowers. You'll recognize your strengths as resources to tap into when faced with a task or decision. And, most importantly, you'll begin to appreciate yourself more for who you *are*, and not who you think you *should* be.

And you'll become more adroit at seeing the superpowers in others—having more respect for your empowered team members. This diversity of strengths is what makes teams dynamic, innovative, and productive. Imagine a team where everyone had the same superpower—like a superhero squad where everyone can fly but no one has super strength, agility, or intellect. Boring! Impractical! It's the unique *blend* of superpowers in a team that enables it to tackle challenges from different angles, find the best solutions and remain dynamic.

After you've identified your superpowers, the real magic happens, as you start applying your strengths to your day-to-day tasks, projects, and goals. This isn't about shoehorning your strengths into everything you do. Rather, it's about intentionally seeking opportunities where you can leverage your strengths toward greater efficiency, enjoyment, and fulfillment.

One more thing before we wrap up this section on individual strengths. Don't fall into the trap of using your superpowers as an excuse to avoid areas where you need growth. Even Superman has his kryptonite. Being strengths-based doesn't mean ignoring those weaknesses. Instead, find ways to *manage* those weaknesses and be aware of your areas for improvement. A great way to do this may be teaming up with someone whose strengths complement yours.

So, harness the force of your personal superpowers. Uncover the hidden gems of your individual strengths. Embrace the journey of self-discovery. Transform your potential into extraordinary performance. The world needs your unique blend of strengths. Your team needs it. You need it. Because, at the end of the day, it's not just about being the best in the world—it's about being the best *for* the world. And that's the magic of strengths.

Strengths Aren't Just Skills

Let's dissect the difference between strengths and skills. Imagine this as an anatomy class, but instead of peering into a biological organism, we're exploring the spiritual body, so to speak, of your unique superpowers.

Strengths and skills? They're just two peas in the same pod, you might be saying. Well, yes and no. Think of them as cousins—related but distinct. Skills are the things you've learned to do well, often through formal training or repeated practice. Strengths, on the other hand, go deeper. They're part of your DNA—your psychological makeup.

Gallup, a leading organization in the field of strengths-based development, distinguishes between the concepts of "talent" and "strength" as follows[2]:

---

[2] The distinctions between "talent" and "strength" are based on concepts from *StrengthsFinder 2.0* by Tom Rath and *Now, Discover Your Strengths* by Buckingham and Clifton, both published by Gallup Press.

Talent: A natural way of thinking, feeling, or behaving. Talents are innate and are the raw materials for strengths. They can be thought of as naturally recurring patterns of thought, feeling, or behavior that can be productively applied. For example, someone might have a natural talent for empathizing with others, meaning that they intuitively sense and understand people's feelings.

Strength: A strength is the ability to consistently provide near-perfect performance in a specific activity. The key to building a strength is to identify your dominant talents, then complement them by acquiring knowledge and skills pertinent to the activity. Strengths are developed when your most powerful talents are refined with practice and combined with acquired knowledge and skills. For example, someone might have a strength in "relationship building" because they have the talent for empathy, which is honed and developed through practice and supplemented with knowledge about effective communication and conflict resolution.

So, essentially, while talent is an innate ability or a natural way of thinking, feeling, or behaving, a strength is the refined and consistent application of that talent, supplemented with knowledge and skills. Here's the definition of what a skill is:

Skill: A skill is the learned ability you possess to carry out a task with pre-determined results, often within a given amount of time, energy, or both. Unlike talents, which are innate, you acquire and develop skills over time through training, practice, and experience. Your skills can be technical, like the ability to code in a specific programming language, or soft, like effective time management. They serve as the bridge between your natural talent and consistent performance, often being the mechanism by which your talent is expressed as a strength. For instance, while you may have a natural talent for visualizing spatial relationships (an innate ability to conceptualize how things will fit together), you might acquire the skill of architectural drafting to harness and express that talent. With further knowledge about building regulations and continual practice, this combination of your talent and skill can be developed into a strength in architectural design.

For example, suppose you're exceptionally good at crunching numbers, and you've got a knack for data analysis and problem solving. This is a skill. But why are you good at it? Maybe it's because you have a strength in analytical thinking. You're naturally curious, you love digging into details, and you enjoy finding patterns and connections that others miss.

See the difference there? The skill is the "what"—it's the specific ability you have. The talent/strength is the "why"—it's the psychological pattern that fuels and informs that ability. Understanding this difference is like flipping the switch on a super-powered spotlight, illuminating the intricate matrix of your superpowers and their interplay with your skills.

Talent, strengths, and skills are all important, and they serve different roles. Skills are like tools in your toolbox. They're handy for specific tasks and situations. Talents and strengths are the hands that wield those tools. They guide how you use your skills, how you learn, and how you interact with others. They influence how you see the world, and they're the driving force behind your actions. Your strengths are the wind beneath your wings, the secret sauce in your superhero sandwich. They're the engine that powers your skills.

Below are some examples that illustrate the distinction between skills (the "what") and talents/strengths (the "why") in a business context.

Jane is a project manager known for her impeccable organizational skills. She can keep multiple projects on track simulta-

neously (the "what" of her skill). But let's delve deeper into the "why." Jane possesses a natural talent for strategic thinking and problem-solving, which she's honed into a strength over time. She has a natural inclination to visualize complex scenarios and anticipate potential issues. Her ability to strategize the best course of action is the driving force behind her skill in project management. So while her organizational skills are the tools, her strategic thinking is the hand that masterfully wields those tools, ensuring that every project she handles is executed efficiently and effectively.

Matt, a successful sales executive renowned for his powers of persuasion, can adeptly convince clients to buy products or services (that's his skill). However, his underlying strength is his innate ability to empathize and connect with others, a strength that he's nurtured over years of interaction and experience. This strength is the fuel that powers his persuasion skills, enabling him to understand clients' needs and helps him to build trust with them. He's able to tailor his communication in a way that resonates with his clients. Therefore, while his persuasion skills are valuable tools, it's his strength in empathy and connection that makes him a standout sales executive.

Interestingly, while skills can become obsolete with technological advances and shifting job markets, strengths are timeless. They're as unique as your fingerprints and as enduring as diamonds. In a rapidly changing world, your strengths provide a reliable compass, guiding your growth and adaptation. They're the magic wand that can turn any situation from mundane to extraordinary.

But here's the kicker: Most people are unaware of their strengths—like unpolished gems, hidden deep within the earth of their subconscious. Our job is to dig them out, polish them, and let them shine. And see an immense transformation—in our performance, our relationships, our well-being, and our overall fulfillment.

Our talents and strengths are the foundation upon which skills are built. They're the magic thread woven through every aspect of our life, our inbuilt superpowers waiting to be harnessed and unleashed. Start mining for those hidden gems, because the world is ready for your unique sparkle.

Transforming Potential into Strengths

Let's unpack some gems from the world of transformation. This is where potential becomes power and everyday straw a golden thread. It's the human magic of turning potential into strengths.

It's like the classic tale of Rumpelstiltskin, only instead of a devious imp spinning straw into gold, it's you—turning raw, unrefined talent into polished strengths. You are Midas himself, engaged in a beautiful alchemy of self-discovery and development.

Let's unpack what we mean by "potential." In this context, potential is the innate ability to grow and excel in a unique capacity. It's the raw material of your talent—your mind's fertile soil, brimming with seeds of greatness. Sounds promising, right? But potential alone is like an un-tuned guitar. It needs to be in tune and a player to make gorgeous music.

That's where strengths come in—honing and finetuning your talents through knowledge and skill building. A strength is what happens when your natural talent meets a focused investment of time and energy. It's like adding water and sunshine to a seed, transforming it into a blossoming flower. It's the art of spinning straw into gold.

You might be thinking, "Sounds all well and good, but how do I turn my potential into strengths? How does this transformation occur?"

First, it's about recognizing your talents, paying attention to what comes naturally to you. What are you drawn to? What do you pick up quickly? It might be a knack for persuasion, an eye for detail, or a mind wired for strategic thinking. It's the stuff that makes you feel alive and charged. And when you do it, you're effortlessly "in the zone."

Then, once you've identified these raw talents, you invest in them. This is where the work comes in. You learn, practice, and hone these talents until they become second nature. This could mean attending workshops, seeking mentorship, taking on challenging projects, or simply dedicating time daily to practice.

Transforming potential into strengths isn't, of course, a quick-fix solution. It's an ongoing journey, requiring patience, dedication, and a good dose of self-love. It's like building a castle brick by brick, or spinning a golden thread inch by inch.

But the effort is well worth the reward. When you turn your potential into strengths, you're not just improving your performance but also boosting your fulfillment and well-being. Work becomes a joy instead of a grind. Challenges become less daunting and more exciting. You stop feeling like a square peg in a round hole, and you start feeling like you're truly in your element.

In the end, spinning straw into gold isn't a fairy tale—it's a feasible reality. It's the magic of turning your untapped potential into tangible strengths. It's the adventure of digging deep within yourself and discovering your unique gems, and then polishing them to a sparkle.

The X-Factor of a Strengths-Based Mindset

Possessing a strengths-based mindset is like the secret sauce, the magic elixir, the X-Factor that supercharges your journey from good to great. A strengths-based mindset is like wearing a pair of magic glasses that lets you see the world—and yourself—through the lens of strengths. You shift your focus from what's wrong to what's strong. Instead of being trapped in a doom-and-gloom mindset, fixating on problems and weaknesses, you zoom in on strengths. If your life's aim is to avoid failure, you'll obsess over rectifying shortcomings. However, if you aspire to flourish, you prioritize enhancing your strengths while navigating around your weaknesses. It's choosing to zero in on what's right with yourself and other people rather than fixating on what's wrong with yourself and others.[3]

Sound too good to be true? Well, it's not a mythical unicorn. It's a real and achievable mindset, backed by a mountain of research in positive psychology.

A strengths-based mindset works like a mental director. Imagine standing on a stage in a bright spotlight. A traditional mindset might have you worried about tripping over the mic wire or forgetting your lines. The strengths-based mindset, however, guides that spotlight to your talent, your passion, and your confidence. The strengths life is not about ignoring the potential pitfalls—it's about empowering you to summon your best performance despite them.

But how do you switch on this mental director, to shine your own spotlight? How do you cultivate a strengths-based mindset? It takes conscious effort and practice.

First, recognize and acknowledge your strengths. Don't just brush them aside with a humble shrug. (Humility is good, but we have to be realistic about who we really are.) Celebrate them! Embrace them! They're your unique superpowers. Use tools like strengths assessments, feedback from others, and self-reflection to identify your strengths.

---

[3] Clifton, D. O., & Harter, J. K. (2003). "Investing in strengths." From K. S. Cameron, J. E. Dutton, & R. E. Quinn (Eds.), *Positive Organizational Scholarship: Foundations of a New Discipline* (pp. 111-121). Berrett-Koehler Publishers.

Next, seek opportunities to leverage your strengths. Whether it's in your daily tasks, projects, or interactions with others, find ways to put your strengths into action. It's like flexing your muscles. The more you use your strengths, the stronger they become and the faster they become perpetual skills.

Also, shift your language to highlight your strengths. Instead of saying "I can't do this," try "I'm great at this other thing. How can I use that to tackle this challenge?" This language (and perception) shift works wonders in solidifying your perspective and boosting your confidence.

And adopt a strengths-based lens toward others. Recognize and appreciate the strengths in your teammates, your colleagues, and your friends. Encourage them to do the same. Learn to see what's right with others first rather than what's wrong with them, fostering a positive, empowering environment where everyone feels valued and motivated.

Cultivating a strengths-based mindset isn't an overnight transformation—it's a gradual and satisfying journey. At times, it'll feel like sailing against the current, as it requires consistent effort and perseverance. But once you get the hang of it, it propels you toward higher performance, bringing greater fulfillment and deepening your connections with others.

The strengths-based mindset is the X-Factor that supercharges your journey to success. It's the illuminating glasses that allow you to see the hidden gems in yourself and others. It's the compass that guides you toward your true north—your unique strengths. So let's put on those glasses, pick up that compass, and embark on the journey of the strengths-based mindset. You've got the X-Factor within you— and now it's time to unleash it.

Team Discussion Questions

1. How would you define your personal superpowers or unique strengths? Can you give an example of a time when you utilized these strengths effectively in your work?

2. The real magic happens when you start applying your strengths to your day-to-day tasks. How can you better integrate your unique strengths into your everyday responsibilities?

3. We emphasize the importance of understanding the difference between skills and strengths. Can you think of any examples in your own experience where understanding this distinction was beneficial?

4. What are some ways you can cultivate a strengths-based mindset within your team? How can this approach influence the team's performance and collaboration?

5. We mention that one's potential can be transformed into strengths. What strategies can you think of to nurture and invest in your raw talents, thus turning them into strengths?

6. How can you apply the concept of a strengths-based mindset when addressing areas for improvement or weaknesses? Can you share any past experiences of when this mindset would have been beneficial?

7. We explore the idea of seeing others through a strengths-based lens. How can we encourage this perspective in our team dynamics, and what impact do you think it would have on our team culture and productivity?

3.
Teams:
The Strengths Laboratory

A team's synergy isn't just about adding diverse strengths; it's about multiplying them. It's synergy on steroids, turning 1+1 into an infinite game changer.

Harmonious Melody—Team Dynamics

Let's dive into the world of team dynamics. Picture each team as a band, with members on different instruments. When distinct notes merge, they create a harmonious melody that's infinitely more captivating than a solo performance. This is the splendor of strengths in team dynamics.

Strengths in a team aren't like ingredients in a salad, where each component retains its distinct identity. They're more like colors in a rainbow or voices in a choir, blending to create a synergistic masterpiece. It's similar to the Avengers ensemble, where the diverse superpowers meld to form an unstoppable force.

So let's figure out who's who, understanding each team member's unique strengths—their "instrument" in the band. One might bring the infectious energy of the drums, while another might possess the soothing melody of the violin. Some have killer guitar riffs. Some team members might excel at creativity (keyboards), others at strategic thinking (bass), while some are great at building relationships (horns).

When people play to their strengths, they bring their A-game to company composition—to harmonious teamwork. They're more engaged, more productive, and more fulfilled. They're like a drummer deep into the groove or a guitarist lost in a solo—performing at peak. Each individual performance boosts the collective performance of the team.

And here's where the maestro—the team leader—enters to ensure that each instrument complements the others. They help to create a space where each member can lean into a graceful flow and use their strengths. They should respect and leverage the strengths of others, too, while ensuring that the drums don't drown the violin and the guitar solos don't overshadow the bass.

This means aligning tasks with strengths, while fostering open communication and encouraging strengths recognition. It means constructively managing conflicts. The maestro creates a "strengths conscious" culture where everyone knows, appreciates, understands, and utilizes their own and each other's strengths. Symbiosis at its best!

This harmonious melody isn't just music to the ears, but it's also rocket fuel for team performance. Research shows that strengths-based teams have lower turnover rates, higher customer satisfaction, and greater profitability.[4] It's like the crowd roaring at a concert—proof of the band's stellar performance.

The melody also strengthens the bonds (harmony) between the team members. It fosters mutual respect and understanding. It accelerates collaboration, transforming a group of individuals into a cohesive, powerhouse team—like a band that jams together, grows together, and creates inspiring and energizing music together.

Strengths have the power to turn team dynamics up to 11, creating a harmonious melody that boosts performance and nurtures relationships. Yes, it's not a solo gig—it's a band performance. As

---

[4] Research findings from various studies, including "Gallup's Q12 Meta-Analysis" and Harter, Schmidt, and Hayes' "The Impact of Strengths-Based Development on Employee Performance Outcomes," show that strengths-based teams have lower turnover rates, higher customer satisfaction, and greater profitability.

we pick up our instruments, we need to tune into each other's strengths, and we'll be amazed at the transformational music.

Synergy on Steroids

So let's explore the incredible power of diverse-strengths integration. This is the realm where 1+1 equals far more than just 2. This is synergy on steroids!

Why do diverse strengths matter? Imagine a soccer team with just goalkeepers, without the strikers, midfielders, and defenders—all with their unique strengths. The same applies to teams in business. You need a mix of visionaries, executors, creatives, analysts, diplomats, and challengers. Each strength is a piece of the puzzle, and it's only when the pieces come together that we see the complete, stunning picture.

Diverse strengths bring diverse perspectives, fueling creative ideas and approaches, resulting in innovative solutions. It's like a creative whirlwind where out-of-the-box ideas fly around wildly and, often, lead to breakthroughs that a homogenous team might not conceive of. It's the secret ingredient that makes the team more than the sum of its parts.

And diverse strengths lead to better decision making. With more angles considered, teams can better foresee potential risks and opportunities, leading to sound, well-rounded decisions. It's like having a GPS that shows all routes, allowing you to choose the best one or combine several to create a new route forward.

And let's not forget about learning. In a strengths-diverse team, members learn from each other, broadening skill sets and perspectives. It's like being in a living, breathing learning lab where everyone grows together.

However, like a multifaceted band, creating synergy from each other's diverse strengths isn't easy (the graveyard of great rock bands is big). It requires an understanding and appreciation of those strengths. Members must tune into the unique frequency of each "instrument" and understand how it adds to the collective melody. This requires a culture of respect. Each strength needs to be valued, not judged. There's no "good" or "bad" strength—only different strengths.

Enter the leader, stage right. They must foster the culture, ensuring that everyone not only knows their own strengths but also appreciates the strengths of their teammates. They orchestrate the sonorous strengths, ensuring that each "instrument" gets its solo while contributing to the collective melody.

And once this synergy hits, it's like a concert amplifier. Projects move faster. Problems get solved creatively. Decisions improve. Job satisfaction soars. It's not just about achieving business goals; it's about growing as individuals and as a team. It's about *enjoying* the game, and not just winning it.

It's time for you to experience this synergy on steroids—to create a masterpiece from the diverse strengths of your team. Yes, it takes all sorts of instruments to create a great band, so let's embrace our diverse strengths and create harmonious human music together.

Nurturing a Strengths-Based Team

Now that we've established the power of a diverse strengths-based team, let's look at nurturing. Like a delicate plant, a strengths-based team needs the right conditions to thrive, so we'll delve into the key ingredients needed to cultivate a flourishing strengths-based team.

Let's start with the "sunlight"—clear communication. Clear and open lines of communication ensure that every team member understands their role, enabling them to grasp the team's goals, and providing a blueprint for how their strengths contribute to achieving those goals. It's not as much about dictating as it is having a heart-to-heart conversation—a chat where everyone is heard, understood, and respected. Think of it like a jam session, where each band member knows their part and how they may contribute to an album.

Next, there's the "water" of team growth—feedback. Regular, constructive feedback helps team members understand how they can shine and improve. But here's the twist: It should focus more on leveraging strengths than on overcoming weaknesses. It's like telling your drummer, "Hey, your rhythm is fantastic! How about adding a bit more energy to the chorus?" It's about watering the seeds of strengths and encouraging them to blossom.

Next up is the "fertilizer"—appreciation and recognition. Everyone craves acknowledgment for their contribution. Celebrating achievements—big and small—and acknowledging how individual strengths contributed to those achievements boosts morale. It encourages team members to keep playing to their strengths. Did your lead guitarist just nail a tricky solo that brought the house down? Make sure she knows what you think!

No garden is complete without the "soil"—trust. In a strengths-based team, it's essential. Team members need to trust each other's abilities, as well as trust the leader to guide them. They need to feel safe to express their thoughts and ideas, knowing that they'll be heard and valued. When leaders foster trust, the roots of collaboration grow stronger, creating a more robust team.

Now, the pièce de resistance: the "gardener"—the team leader. They set the tone for a strengths-based culture and must embody a like mindset. The leader needs to focus on what's strong, not on what's wrong. They focus on accelerating team strengths. They create opportunities for each team member to use their strengths and ensure that the whole team understands and values the strengths of each person. A great leader isn't a "boss" but a "conductor," orchestrating the strengths band to create beautiful music.

Nurturing a strengths-based team is a deliberate and continuous process—not a one-off. It's a journey of discovery, growth, and camaraderie. It's about creating an environment where everyone can be their best selves, where strengths aren't just recognized but celebrated. It's a culture where everyone is encouraged to grow, and where the team is more than just the sum of its parts.

But, most importantly, it's about enjoying the journey. So many things go right when you enjoy the music you create together. After all, when a team becomes a band of strength maestros, work be-comes less of a chore and more of a jam session—where everyone brings their unique "instrument" and plays to their strengths. To-gether, they create a melody that's music to everyone's ears.

Team Discussion Questions

1. In your team, what unique strength does each member bring, and how do they blend to create a harmonious whole? Discuss some specific instances where these came into play in a project or task.

2. How can the team leader ensure that each team member's unique strengths are being used optimally and complement one another? Share some experiences or challenges you've had in this area.

3. What are some strategies that can be implemented to foster an environment of open communication and strength recognition? How can we better incorporate these into our team's culture?

4. Why is a diversity of strengths important in a team, and how has this diversity led to innovative solutions or improved decision making in your team? Are there any areas where our team could benefit from more diversity?

5. What role does feedback play in a strengths-based team, and how can it be delivered constructively to focus more on leveraging strengths rather than on overcoming weaknesses?

6. How can trust be cultivated within a team to foster collaboration and better utilize each other's strengths? Discuss any instances where trust (or lack of trust) significantly affected team performance.

7. How can we create a continuous culture of celebrating and leveraging our strengths in the team? What initiatives or practices could to help make the recognition of strengths a regular part of our team's workflow?

4.
Strengths-Based Leadership: The Magnetic Catalyst

Strengths-based leadership is the magnetic field
in the talent market, attracting unique abilities and
sculpting them into compelling masterpieces.

Attracting and Cultivating Talent

As we explore strengths-based leadership, we'll see how it doesn't just attract talent—it cultivates it. Get ready to turn your leadership dial to "attract" and become a magnetic force in the talent market.

Imagine that you are a promising talent in the business world. You're searching for a job that's more than just a paycheck. You're yearning for a place where you can unleash your full potential, somewhere that values you for what you're great at. Then, you stumble upon a company that talks not just about targets and revenue but about strengths, growth, and thriving. Now, that's a magnetic pull!

Strengths-based leadership works like a magnet, attracting talent that craves a meaningful work environment. Such leadership signals a culture where people are seen, heard, and valued—an environment that puts employees first. When you as a leader focus on strengths, you're not just saying, "We want you for your skills." You're saying, "We want you for who you are, and we believe that you can do great things." That's a message that resonates deeply with today's emerging talent.

But attraction is only half the story. The other half is about cultivating that talent—helping them grow, flourish, and stay. This is where strengths-based leadership shines. By focusing on strengths, you're providing fertile soil where people can plant their unique seeds and watch them blossom. You're creating an environment where colleagues can build upon their natural abilities and become the best versions of themselves.

To do this, you invest in your team, providing them with opportunities to learn, grow, and develop. This may mean targeted training, mentorship programs, or simply providing challenging projects that incentivize people to leverage strengths. You might be the lead vocalist, but your bassist may play an amazing solo. Give them the spotlight and watch them nail it!

Fostering a strengths-based culture means providing regular and meaningful feedback. This celebrates successes, acknowledges effort, and provides constructive input. It's about having ongoing conversations about strengths and how they can be leveraged further. It's not a one-off performance review but a continuous dialogue—a jam session of ideas, if you will.

And most importantly, cultivating talent requires genuine care and concern for people's well-being. This means respecting work-life harmony, promoting a positive work environment, and supporting employees in times of difficulty. You understand that each team member is a person first and an employee second. Your drummer may have had a bad day. Show her empathy, offer support—and you can bet that she'll drum better than ever tomorrow.

Attracting and cultivating talent isn't a one-and-done strategy. It's an ongoing process and a never-ending concert, requiring commitment, patience, and a deep belief in people's potential. It's about creating a magnetic pull that attracts talent to a nurturing environment that encourages them to stay, grow, and thrive.

Unleashing the Lions

Now let's dive into the topic of unleashing the lions and empowering your team to excel. It's time to hear the roar of talents reaching their peak performance and discover how a strengths-based leader is integral to this journey.

Imagine a pride of lions, each with unique strengths. One has an eagle eye for spotting prey that's miles away, another is lightning quick, and yet another possesses a strategic mind for complex hunting. Each brings a distinct strength to the hunt, making the pride stronger and more capable. Just like our lion pride, each member of your team has unique strengths that make the team more effective.

Strengths-based leadership is about unlocking these strengths and empowering each "lion" in your team. You enable people to do what they do best every day. The result? A highly engaged team, roaring with motivation, brimming with creativity, and ready to take on any challenge that comes their way.

But how does one go about unleashing these lions? The answer lies in three key elements: recognition, autonomy, and opportunities for growth.

Recognition of individual strengths is the first step. You assess each team member's unique abilities and how they can contribute to team success. After a while, you know which lion in your pride is the fastest runner or the best strategist. By acknowledging and validating these strengths, you fuel self-confidence, spark motivation, and instill a sense of value in your team members. Every "lion" wants to know they're an integral part of the pride. (They take pride in that fact.)

Next, autonomy. Like lions need room to roam, team members require space to exercise their strengths. Micromanagement can be as stifling as a small cage for a mighty lion. Instead, give your team the freedom to use their strengths in ways they deem fit. This not only enhances their sense of responsibility but also allows them to innovate, problem-solve, and achieve individual excellence.

Finally, provide growth opportunities. The savannah is a vast place with new experiences around every turn or grove, and lions love exploring it. Similarly, team members love challenges that stretch their capabilities and allow them to grow. By providing such opportunities, you encourage your "lions" to amplify their strengths, learn new skills, and strive for greater personal and professional development.

Empowerment isn't about stepping back completely. You provide guidance when needed, support in times of struggle, and you celebrate successes together. It's about striking a balance between giving freedom and offering support. It's an intricate dance, and it's crucial that a strengths-based leader masters it.

Unleashing the lions isn't just about maximizing performance. You're fostering an environment where each team member feels valued, capable, and motivated—creating a pride that's not just successful but also cohesive, supportive, and resilient. So, brace yourselves, leaders! It's time to release the lions within your team.

Next, let's explore how a strengths-based leader encourages both growth through strengths and moving beyond the comfort zone—because even the fiercest lion must push its boundaries to thrive.

Beyond the Comfort Zone

In the terrain beyond the comfort zone is where the real magic of strengths-based leadership reveals itself. Let's explore how leaders can encourage growth through strengths, challenging their teams to unleash their full potential.

Navigating this terrain requires understanding that true growth happens when we're willing to take risks. Just like a lion pushing its limits to reach new hunting grounds, we expand our capacity when we're willing to approach the edges of uncertainty. Being comfortable is pleasant, but it often means staying stagnant. As a strengths-based leader, your goal is to gently nudge your team out of their comfort zones—toward the creative edges. They need us to promote a team culture where growth and learning are encouraged and celebrated.

So you first cultivate an environment that encourages taking calculated risks. Even lions must venture into unknown territory to find prey. Encourage your team to take tasks that push their boundaries and expand their skills—anything from leading a new project, venturing into a new market, or even learning a new technology. The key here is to make certain that these challenges align with their strengths. This creates a sense of excitement rather than fear. And when they succeed? Shower them with recognition. Make it a roaring celebration of their achievement and courage to venture beyond the familiar.

With your risk environment in place, you can now foster a "growth mindset." This term, coined by psychologist Carol Dweck, means believing that abilities can be developed and improved.[5] In our lion analogy, it means knowing that even the smallest cub can grow into a mighty hunter with practice and persistence. As a leader, promote the idea that failures are opportunities to learn, and that mistakes are stepping stones to success. Encourage your team to view challenges as chances to amplify their strengths rather than threats to be avoided.

Lastly, a leader must know that growth doesn't always come from tackling new challenges. Sometimes, it comes from deepening existing strengths. Again, think of a lion, perfecting its hunting technique until it becomes second nature. Similarly, provide your

---

[5] Dweck, Carol S., *Mindset: The New Psychology of Success*. Ballantine Books, 2006. Dweck presents the concept of a "growth mindset" and contrasts it with a "fixed mindset," explaining the profound impact these mindsets have on personal and professional development.

team with opportunities to refine their strengths. Make them true masters in their field. Encourage them to attend workshops, take advanced courses, and mentor others. This reinforces their existing strengths and boosts confidence, further enticing them beyond their comfort zone.

Throughout this process, you provide support and guidance. Just as the leader of a lion pride keeps a protective eye on its members while they explore new territories, you are there for your team. Offer constructive feedback, lend a helping hand when they stumble, and, above all, encourage them to keep going.

Venturing beyond the comfort zone isn't easy—sometimes fraught with uncertainty and potential setbacks—but the rewards are invaluable. By encouraging growth through strengths, you're not only elevating your team's performance but also building their resilience, confidence, and adaptability. You're creating a team of lions ready to conquer any savannah or jungle.

Up next, we'll dive into the ocean of strengths-based organizations. This is where the ripples of individual and team strengths create a tidal wave of organizational success. Until then, keep encouraging your team to roar louder, leap further, and aim higher.

Team Discussion Questions

1. How can we as a team better recognize and validate individual strengths to fuel self-confidence and motivation?

2. In what ways could we be stifling individual strengths through micromanagement? How can we give more autonomy to our team members to use their strengths in ways they deem fit?

3. What opportunities for growth are currently available to our team? How can we create more opportunities that allow each member to stretch their capabilities and enhance their strengths?

4. How can we cultivate an environment that encourages taking calculated risks? Can you think of any examples of how stepping outside of a comfort zone might benefit us individually and as a team?

5. How can we promote a growth mindset within our team, viewing failures and mistakes as stepping stones to success and learning opportunities?

6. Are there areas where we could refine and deepen our existing strengths? How could we make this a priority?

7. What are some ways that we as a team can support each other in venturing beyond our comfort zones, offering constructive feedback and encouragement? How can we better cultivate resilience, confidence, and adaptability within our team?

5.
Strengths-Based Organizations: The Revolution

In this strengths-based revolution, we're not simply building organizations; we're cultivating thriving ecosystems, where every individual contribution becomes the heartbeat of collective success.

The Strengths-Based Ecosystem

The terrain of strengths-based organizations is reshaping the business world. To navigate this landscape, we'll need to understand the intricate workings of the strengths-based ecosystem. Let's explore the interconnected layers of this dynamic environment.

A strengths-based ecosystem is a vibrant, living entity, much like a rainforest teeming with diverse species—each with unique strengths contributing to the forest's overall health and prosperity. This ecosystem, when applied to organizations, comprises various elements: individuals, teams, leadership, and culture—all interlinked and interdependent, forming an organic, thriving whole.

At the heart of this ecosystem are individuals. Just like every tree in a rainforest is unique, so is each person in your organization, bringing a distinctive set of strengths—the natural talents that energize them and in which they excel. These strengths serve as the lifeblood of the ecosystem, pulsating through the organization and fueling its growth.

Teams form the next layer of the ecosystem. When individuals unite, their strengths interact and intermingle. It's like how different plant species form a robust undergrowth. Each team member's strengths complement the strengths of others, which leads to more innovative solutions, increased resilience, and enhanced productivity—like a forest, where the variety of trees and plants makes it stronger and more resilient.

Then we have leaders—the towering trees of our rainforest metaphor. These leaders aren't just managers, but also the custodians of the strength's philosophy. Their job is to identify, nurture, and leverage the strengths of their team members. They set the tone, encourage strengths-based behaviors, and advocate for a work environment where every individual feels valued for their unique contributions.

Lastly, like a rainforest thriving in a balanced climate, a strengths-based ecosystem thrives in the right culture—one that champions strengths, celebrates diverse talents, encourages continuous growth, and fosters a sense of camaraderie. It's a culture where every person feels empowered to be their authentic selves, and a place where everyone is recognized for their distinct strengths.

Within this vibrant ecosystem, there's a free flow of energy and nutrients. Individuals are more engaged, and they're more fulfilled because they're utilizing their strengths. Teams perform optimally as the diverse strengths of their members complement each other. Leaders successfully drive results by harnessing the collective strengths. The culture, infused with the strength's philosophy, promotes innovation, collaboration, and resilience. The whole organization becomes a living entity, pulsating with the vibrant energy of strengths.

Understanding how a strengths-based ecosystem operates is crucial because it allows us to see its extraordinary possibilities, providing a blueprint for reshaping organizations into thriving, dynamic entities. Each individual, team member, and leader contributes their unique strengths to the overall success. It's a revolution in the way we view and conduct business, and it's poised to redefine the future of work.

This is the strengths-based ecosystem in action—an interconnected web of individuals, teams, and leaders, a strengths-centric culture that creates an organization that's not just surviving but thriving. As we cultivate a strengths-based organization, we'll experience the powerful benefits of this ecosystem and how it transforms the business world.

Southwest Airlines

A prime example of a strengths-based organization is Southwest Airlines. It has long been lauded for its unique corporate culture, which aligns with the strengths-based ecosystem.

Southwest places immense value on the uniqueness of every employee. They often say that they hire for attitude and train for skill, emphasizing the inherent strengths and natural talents of individuals. They believe that technical aspects can be trained, but individual strengths like a positive attitude, empathy, and a team spirit are innate and invaluable.

Within the realm of teams, much like the dense undergrowth in a forest, Southwest's teams are built on a foundation of trust and mutual respect. The airline's operational success can be attributed to teams that leverage the diverse strengths of their members. From ground crews to flight attendants, teams are cross-trained and empowered to make decisions, capitalizing on each member's strengths for collective benefit.

Southwest's leaders, akin to the towering trees in our ecosystem analogy, act as guardians of the airline's unique culture. They lead with humility and prioritize the well-being of employees. Leaders like former CEO Herb Kelleher were known for their hands-on approach and genuine interest in recognizing and nurturing the strengths of employees.

Southwest's culture resonates with the strengths-based ecosystem's principles. Their motto, "Employees come first, customers second," frankly shows that if they cater to the strengths and needs of their employees, those employees will, in turn, provide unmatched service to the customers. It's a culture of mutual respect, recognition, and continuous growth.

It stands as a testament to a strengths-based ecosystem not being just a theoretical concept. It's a practical, profitable, and sustainable approach to business. When organizations like Southwest champion the individual strengths of their members and promote a cohesive, strengths-centric culture, they deservedly soar to great heights in their industry.

Powering Success

Having explored the intricate workings of a strengths-based ecosystem, it's time to discuss how this revolutionary approach powers success. Let's dive into the compelling business case for strengths-based organizations.

A strengths-based organization isn't merely an abstract concept of empowerment; it's a transformative blueprint for achieving real-world success. Like harnessing the wind to power a sailboat, leaders use the natural talents and abilities of individuals to propel an organization forward. But why is this approach so powerful? What's the business case justifying it? Let's explore further.

First, there's employee engagement. Like the winds filling the sails, engaged employees drive organizational success. Gallup research shows that teams focusing on their strengths are more engaged, and highly engaged teams produce 21% higher profitability. When employees have the chance to do what they do best every day, they're more productive and more likely to stay with their organization.[6]

[6] Gallup's State of the Global Workplace reports: These reports provide insights and statistics about employee engagement worldwide.

Second, a strengths-based approach supercharges team performance. A study by the Corporate Leadership Council revealed that when organizations concentrate on employees' strengths, performance can increase by up to 36%. Why? Because teams that understand and leverage their diverse strengths can collaborate more effectively. They come up with more innovative solutions and can better navigate challenges.[7]

Third, the strengths-based approach boosts leadership effectiveness. Research by Zenger Folkman shows that leaders who leverage their strengths are more successful and likelier to excel in their roles. These leaders create a positive domino effect throughout the organization, encouraging others to play to their strengths and seek exceptional business outcomes.[8]

And then there is what every company must be aware of—the bottom line. A report by the Human Capital Institute and the VIA Institute on Character showed organizations focusing on strengths had, on average, 14% higher net profit margins and a 9% increase in sales. A strengths-based organization is good for its people—*and* for its profits.[9]

Finally, consider the long-term implications. In our fast-paced world, businesses must adapt or face extinction. The strengths-based approach fosters a culture of continuous learning and development, promoting agility and resilience. By focusing on strengths, organizations better navigate the changing business landscape, ensuring survival and success in the long run.

---

[7] The Corporate Leadership Council is part of the Corporate Executive Board (CEB), which was later acquired by Gartner. They conduct various research projects and studies focused on best practices in management and leadership.

[8] See Zenger Folkman's research and its book, *The Extraordinary Leader: Turning Good Managers into Great Leaders* for insights on strengths-based leadership.

[9] For more on this topic, see the Human Capital Institute (HCI) at www.hci.org for talent management insights and the VIA Institute on Character at www.viacharacter.org for studies on character strengths.

Adobe Systems

Imagine bustling Silicon Valley, home to tech giants and startups, each vying to create the next groundbreaking product. Amid this competitive breeding ground, Adobe Systems stands out, not just for its software products but also for its adoption of a strengths-based approach. Here's how the company has championed the principles we've been exploring.

Adobe's leadership recognizes the intrinsic value of tapping into the natural talents of its vast employee base. Shantanu Narayen, Adobe's CEO, didn't merely adopt a strengths-based mindset; he championed it. Much like the principle of embracing strengths at the leadership level, he ensured that his leadership approach was infused with it. By leveraging his strengths in vision, strategy, and execution, he set the tone for the rest of the company.

This focus trickled down and led to higher employee engagement. Adobe teams, passionate about their work and aware of their individual strengths, became powerhouses of innovation. The company's regular Adobe Kickbox initiative, for instance, empowered employees by giving them resources and freedom to pursue innovative ideas, amplifying their inherent strengths.

The principle of enhanced team performance? Adobe's a living testament. The company's commitment to strengths has cultivated teams that collaborate seamlessly. Its design and engineering teams often come together, integrating unique strengths, resulting in products that are both technically robust and aesthetically unparalleled.

Adobe's leadership also thrives in this environment. They aren't just appointed based on tenure or technical prowess but also on their ability to harness and champion the strengths of their teams. This leadership style reverberates through the organization, encouraging a culture where strengths are identified, celebrated, and utilized to their fullest.

Financially, while exact figures tying directly to its strengths-based approach might be proprietary, Adobe's consistent growth, market dominance, and high employee retention rates speak volumes. It's evident that a strengths-focused culture doesn't just boost morale—it significantly impacts the bottom line.

Adobe's commitment to fostering a culture of continuous learning, driven by individual strengths, ensures that it remains at the forefront of innovation. As technology evolves, Adobe remains agile, resilient, and ever-adaptive, echoing the belief that a strengths-based approach isn't just a short-term strategy but a long-term vision. As you envision transforming your own organization, draw inspiration from Adobe—whose journey showcases the immense power of a strengths-based approach in a tangible, impactful manner.

As we've seen, the business case for strengths-based organizations is compelling. It's backed by substantial evidence, and it's a win-win situation, benefiting individuals, teams, and the organization itself. It's like a finely tuned orchestra, where each musician plays to their strengths, creating a harmonious performance that delights the audience and propels the orchestra to new heights. The future is strengths-based, and it's brighter than ever.

Creating a Strengths-Based Culture

A strengths-based culture provides the most dynamic advantage in an alchemic business environment. It's a powerful approach that can revolutionize your own business success. So how can you mold an organizational culture that breathes and thrives on strengths?

First thing's first—let's demystify the term "culture." Think of culture as the invisible yet tangible DNA of an organization. It's the shared set of beliefs, behaviors, and norms that subtly guide how individuals and teams work together. It's how people *feel* when they show up and work together. A strengths-based culture, then, is one where everyone recognizes, values, and leverages their own and each other's strengths. So how do we create such a culture? How can we turn this imagined utopia into reality? Here's a step-by-step approach:

1. **Embrace the strengths mindset at the top.** Like a river, a strengths-based culture starts at the source—its leadership. Leaders not only endorse but genuinely embody this approach. They recognize and leverage their own strengths while appreciating the diverse strengths of their team.

2. **Spread the strengths language.** Introduce the strengths terminology into your organization's dialect. Use strengths assessments, provide training, and weave strengths-based language into your everyday discussions, meetings, and performance reviews. This will ensure that everyone speaks and understands the same strengths language—and cultivate a shared perspective.

3. **Foster strengths recognition.** Encourage individuals and teams to recognize and celebrate each other's strengths regularly. This could be through formal recognition programs or spontaneous acts of appreciation. When people feel seen and valued for their strengths, they're more likely to lean into them.

4. **Tailor roles and teams around strengths.** Where possible, tailor roles to suit individuals' strengths. Form diverse teams where everyone's strengths complement each other, ensuing that everyone gets to do what they do best, which, in turn, boosts productivity and satisfaction.

5. **Encourage strengths development.** Promote a growth mindset. Encourage employees to explore, develop, and leverage their strengths in new ways. This could be through strengths-focused development plans, coaching, or providing opportunities to stretch and grow strengths.

6. **Embed strengths in your processes.** Integrate the strengths' philosophy into your processes and systems, such as recruitment, onboarding, training, and performance management. This ensures that the strengths-based approach isn't just a standalone initiative but woven into the fabric of your organization.

Creating a strengths-based culture isn't a one-time project; it's a continuous journey, requiring commitment, patience, and resilience. But, as many organizations have discovered, the rewards are well worth the effort. It's the ultimate game changer, creating an environment where everyone thrives, engagement soars, and performance skyrockets. It's like a lush, thriving forest, where every tree contributes uniquely to the ecosystem's richness.

As we journey further into the world of strengths-based organizations, we'll equip you with practical tools to unleash the power of strengths in your teams and individuals. The strengths revolution is in full swing, and we're just getting started.

Team Discussion Questions

1. How do the unique strengths of everyone contribute to the overall health and success of your business team?

2. Discuss the role of leadership in a strengths-based organization. How can leaders become more than just managers—instead becoming the custodians of the strengths philosophy?

3. In the strengths-based ecosystem, the culture champions diverse talent and encourages continuous growth. What steps can your team take to create a work environment that fosters this type of culture?

4. Considering the idea of a strengths-based ecosystem, how do you envision the flow of energy within your team? How could this model increase engagement and productivity within your business unit?

5. The business case for a strengths-based approach includes increased employee engagement, supercharged team performance, and boosted leadership effectiveness. How can you implement this approach in your current work situation?

6. What are some practical ways you could start integrating a strengths-based culture into your organization's processes and systems, such as recruitment, onboarding, training, and performance management?

7. A strengths-based culture is considered the ultimate game changer in this revolution. What challenges do you anticipate in implementing such a culture, and how would you address them?

6.
Getting Practical:
A Strengths-Based Toolkit

The Strengths Gym isn't a place of mirrors and
machines but a realm where the heaviest lifting
happens in the mind as you flex and
cultivate your inner talents.

Unleashing Your Inner Strengths Detective

In our quest to master the strengths-based approach, we've reached
a crucial juncture. The path ahead requires us to pull out our tool-
kit of strengths identification techniques—to unearth the hidden
gems within us and our teams.

Every journey of discovery begins with a sense of curiosity, and
identifying strengths is no different. We explore the less-traveled
paths, requiring a mindset shift and a willingness to look beyond
the obvious. We must learn to appreciate the uniqueness in ourselves and others, and about find the extraordinary in the ordinary.
Let's examine some techniques to help us unlock these secrets.

1. **Strengths assessment tools.** Begin your strengths journey with the help of scientifically backed strengths assessment tools, such as the CliftonStrengths, StandOut, or
   VIA Character Strengths survey. They are like your trusty
   magnifying glass—helping you get a clear, in-depth view
   of your natural patterns of thinking, feeling, and behaving.

2. **Feedback analysis.** Sherlock Holmes had his network of
   informants, and as a Strengths Detective, you have your
   colleagues, family, and friends. Ask them about the times
   when they've seen you at your best. This feedback can un-

cover strengths that you might've overlooked or undervalued.

3. **Strengths journaling.** Keep a strengths diary, and jot down instances when you felt particularly energized and fulfilled at work. You'll see patterns emerge, and these are signals of your strengths. It's like collecting clues—each one bringing you closer to uncovering your true strengths.

4. **Job crafting.** Reflect on how you naturally tweak your tasks and responsibilities to suit your preferences and skills. This self-adjusting process is known as job crafting, and it can reveal your intrinsic strengths.

5. **Look for recurring themes.** Pay attention to themes in your life and work, such as tasks you always volunteer for, topics you love learning about, and activities you lose track of time doing. These themes often point to your underlying strengths.

6. **Strengths interview.** Conduct or participate in a structured interview focused on past achievements and gratifying experiences. Analyzing these instances can help to highlight the strengths that contributed to your success.

7. **Visualization techniques.** Imagine your ideal day at work. Think through your tasks, interactions, and achievements. Visualizing this provides insights into your strengths, as our ideals often align with our inherent capabilities.

Like any seasoned detective, you'll realize that no single method is comprehensive—each with its strengths (pun intended) and limitations. The secret lies in using a combination of these methods to triangulate and validate your findings.

Setting out with you inner Strengths Detective begins an exhilarating and revealing journey. You'll discover not only your strengths but also your passion and purpose. And you'll start to more greatly appreciate the diversity of strengths around you, which leads to richer relationships and more fulfilling collaborations.

The Strengths Gym

As we continue our strengths-based adventure, let's venture into the Strengths Gym and explore activities to boost individual strengths. Here are some activities designed to flex and boost your individual strengths.

1. **Strength spotting.** Just like an athlete recognizes and hones their physical skills, a strength spotter identifies and develops their mental talents. Pay close attention to the tasks that energize you. Where do you lose track of time or consistently excel? This isn't a one-and-done activity; it's a lifelong habit of noticing and nurturing your strengths.

2. **Job crafting.** Job crafting doubles as a workout too. By tweaking your job to better align with your strengths, you're not only unearthing your hidden talents but also giving them a regular workout—for an absolute win-win.

3. **Mentoring and coaching.** Just as a personal trainer customizes your workout, a mentor or coach helps you to develop your strengths to full potential. They provide constructive feedback, guide you through challenges, and celebrate your successes. Their experience can effectively help you to navigate the strength-development journey.

4. **Strengths reflection.** Allocate time each week to reflect on how you've used your strengths. What went well? What could be improved? This exercise encourages you to think about your strengths proactively. How can you use your strengths more intentionally?

5. **Strengths challenges.** Set weekly challenges based on your strengths. If "Creativity" is one of your strengths, challenge yourself to come up with a new idea or solution every day. This not only strengthens your abilities but also provides you with tangible examples of how you can apply your strengths in different contexts.

6. **Team activities.** Participate in team activities to exercise diverse strengths. Group projects, brainstorming sessions, and team-building exercises encourage members to use their unique strengths—stepping outside the box—giving you a chance to see how different strengths interact and complement each other.

7. **Continual learning.** Commit to learning more about your strengths. Read books. Attend workshops. Listen to podcasts. The more you understand your strengths, the better you utilize them.

8. **Praise and recognition.** Lastly, don't forget the power of positive reinforcement. When you use your strengths effectively, acknowledge your success. Self-praise is a great motivator, helping to reinforce the behaviors that lead to success.

The Strengths Gym is an ongoing growth-journey. It's a path to experiment, to fail, to learn, and to rise stronger. It's not about being the best but about being your best self. The focus isn't about eliminating weaknesses; it's about amplifying strengths so that they overshadow potential limitations.

Building and Sustaining a Strengths Team

Just as a symphony requires each instrument to play its part for the grand orchestra to create harmonious music, so too does a team need each member to utilize their strengths to work together constructively.

Let's try a different analogy. Think of a strengths-based team as a jigsaw puzzle. Each piece is unique but when put together, they create a beautiful and complete picture. For such a team to thrive and attain the big picture, we need to focus on two key factors: building the team on strengths and then sustaining its energy, power and cohesiveness.

Building a Strengths-Based Team:

- **Hire for strengths.** As tempting as it is to hire a jack-of-all-trades, focusing on strengths-based hiring is more beneficial in the long run. Seek candidates whose strengths align with the job requirements and the team's needs.

- **Gain awareness of strengths.** Ensure that each team member knows their strengths and those of their teammates. Consider organizing a strengths-awareness workshop, or share tools and resources to help employees identify strengths.

- **Design roles around strengths.** As much as possible, design or tailor roles around individual strengths. Encourage employees to use their strengths daily, to foster satisfaction and productivity.

Sustaining a Strengths-Based Team:

- **Provide regular strengths check-ins.** Foster an environment where strengths are discussed regularly, not just during performance reviews. Weekly or monthly check-ins where employees can share how they've used their strengths builds a positive team culture.

- **Promote strengths development.** Encourage and provide resources for continuous strengths development. This might include workshops, coaching sessions, or even online courses. Strengths are like muscles; they need regular exercise to grow.

- **Celebrate strengths.** Make it a habit to celebrate when team members use their strengths effectively. This reinforces the importance of using strengths, and it helps employees to feel valued.

- **Lead by example.** As a leader, use your strengths and talk about them. When employees see you walking the strengths-talk, they're more inclined to mirror you.

- **Encourage collaboration around strengths.** Encourage projects where team members can synergize their strengths. This not only boosts creativity and productivity but also helps team members to appreciate each other's strengths.

- **Resolve conflict using strengths.** Use strengths as a framework for resolving conflicts. Understanding each other's strengths helps to clarify misunderstandings, as it promotes constructive dialogue.

- **Give strengths-based feedback.** Focus on strengths when giving feedback. Highlighting how employees can use their strengths to address areas of improvement is far more motivating than focusing on weaknesses.

Creating and sustaining a strengths-based team is like conducting your own symphony. It requires attentiveness, precision, and a deep understanding of each instrument. And the result is a harmonious melody of collaboration and success—worthy of your protean effort.

Team Discussion Questions

1. Can you share an instance when using one of your strengths led to a successful outcome? How did this experience impact you and the result?

2. In what ways have you integrated the feedback from colleagues or family to identify or confirm your strengths?

3. What trends have you noticed while journaling about your strengths? What surprised you?

4. How have you modified your role to better leverage your strengths? Can you provide an example?

5. Identify recurring activities or roles at work to which you naturally gravitate. What strengths do they indicate?

6. How do you plan to utilize Strengths Gym activities to nurture and apply your strengths? Can you share a specific action plan for the upcoming week?

7. As a team, how can we better acknowledge and celebrate the effective use of individual strengths to enhance team morale and productivity?

7.
Onboarding New Members: The Strengths Way

When we onboard new team members, we aren't just introducing them to a job; we're unlocking the door to their unique strengths and inviting them to flourish.

The Strengths Express

In this section, we'll be exploring the onboarding process in a strengths-based team. This process helps new team members to understand their value and to find their place within the team quickly and effectively. Here are five steps in the process.

1. **Orientation.** Orientation isn't just about company policies or job roles; it's also about familiarizing new hires with the team's strengths landscape. Introduce them to the concept of strengths-based work and give them a snapshot of the team's collective strengths. This provides a clear window into the team's dynamics and how their unique strengths will contribute to the unique ecosystem.

2. **Strengths assessment.** A vital step in the strengths-based onboarding journey is helping newcomers to identify their strengths. Use established tools like the CliftonStrengths assessment, StandOut, or VIA Character Strengths survey. Conducting these assessments early helps new hires to understand their superpowers, and it clears a path forward for their (and the team's) success. The earlier they start leveraging their strengths, the quicker they'll be able to contribute meaningfully to the team.

3. **Strengths introduction.** Allow new team members to share their strengths with the rest of the team. This not only helps everyone to understand the newcomer's strengths but also sets the stage for potential collaborations based on complementary strengths. It can be as formal as a presentation or as informal as a team lunch or coffee chat.

4. **Strengths mentorship.** Assign a mentor to each new hire. The mentor should have a firm grasp of the strengths-based approach, so they can provide guidance on how to apply strengths in daily work, offer insights based on their experiences, and serve as a sounding board for ideas and questions.

5. **Strengths integration.** The last step is integrating new members into the team. When assigning initial tasks or projects, keep their strengths in mind. This shows that you value their unique capabilities and are keen to leverage them. This also helps to boost their confidence and expedite their settling in.

A strengths-based onboarding process is a potent tool for quickly creating an inclusive and engaging work environment, showing new hires that they're valued for both their role and *who* they are. Essentially, it accelerates the process of new members morphing into productive team players.

This onboarding takes a lot of work, but the payoff is worth it. When new team members are onboarded the strengths way, they're likely to settle in faster, be more engaged, and contribute more quickly. And they'll be well on their way to becoming a fully-fledged member of your symphony of strengths.

Nurturing the Saplings

Like a sapling needing the right nutrients and care to grow into a sturdy tree, the care for new team members is a crucial aspect of building a strengths-based organization. The onboarding process might've planted the seeds of strengths awareness, but it's the continued nourishment that'll transform those seeds into towering trees of productivity and engagement. Here are some practical tips on how to help new colleagues blossom in a strengths culture.

1. **Watering the roots: reinforcement of strengths.** For new hires, the concept of strengths-based work might initially be new and slightly challenging, so continuous reinforcement of the strengths perspective is critical. Regular one-on-one discussions about their strengths, and how they've used them in their work, reinforces the concept and encourages new hires to consciously apply their strengths. Recognize and celebrate them when they accomplish this—creating a positive feedback loop that boosts their confidence and engagement levels.

2. **Providing the right environment: strengths-based culture.** Just like a sapling requires the right conditions to thrive, so does a new team member. The right condition is a strengths-based culture. Encourage the entire team to adopt a strengths-based language and approach in their interactions. When team members consistently and openly acknowledge and appreciate each other's strengths, it normalizes strengths discussions and makes them part of the team's DNA.

3. **Pruning for growth: coaching and development.** Professional development in a strengths-based team should revolve primarily around enhancing strengths rather than fixing weaknesses. Strengths-based coaching is an effective tool here. Regular coaching sessions help new hires to better understand their strengths, to learn how to apply them

in different scenarios, and to plan their professional growth path based on their strengths. This approach not only aligns with their natural inclinations but also motivates them to improve continuously.

4. **Strengths pairing: encouraging collaboration.** One of the most effective ways to cultivate strengths is by pairing team members with complementary strengths, encouraging learning from each other and facilitating innovative problem-solving. It also builds strong relationships within the team, improving collaboration and overall team cohesion.

5. **The right nutrition: learning opportunities.** Offer learning opportunities tailored to individual strengths. For example, if someone has the "Learner" strength, provide them with resources to further plumb their field of interest. If another person has the "relator" strength, provide opportunities to build deep relationships within the team. Personalizing learning experiences based on strengths not only boosts skills but also increases engagement and satisfaction levels.

6. **Weathering the storms: resilience building.** The early days in a new job can be challenging, so leveraging strengths can be an effective resilience-building tool. Help new hires identify which strengths can help them to cope with challenges. For instance, someone with the "Positivity" strength might be able to keep their spirits high in a stressful situation, while someone with the "Strategic" strength might find alternative solutions to a problem.

In a strengths-based team, every new hire is a sapling with the potential to grow into a majestic tree, contributing significantly to the success and vibrancy of the organization. But for this transformation to happen, it's crucial to nurture the sapling carefully and provide it with the right care and environment.

Team Discussion Questions

1. How can we better tailor our orientation process to highlight the concept of strengths-based work, as well as introduce new team members to our collective strengths?

2. What are some methods we can use to help new hires identify and understand their strengths as early as possible in their onboarding journey?

3. How can we encourage new team members to share their strengths with the rest of the team in a way that fosters understanding and potential collaboration?

4. What qualities should we look for in a mentor to ensure that they can effectively guide new hires in applying their strengths in their work?

5. How can we incorporate a new hire's unique strengths when assigning them initial tasks or projects?

6. What strategies can we employ to regularly reinforce the strengths perspective for our new hires, and how can we celebrate their effective use of strengths?

7. What are some ways we can cultivate a strengths-based culture within the team to provide the right environment for new hires to thrive?

8.
The Strengths Impact:
Leaders and Organizations

A strengths-based approach doesn't just light up the
organization from within; it sets a beacon for the
entire world, declaring that the future is indeed bright.

It's Global

As we lift our gaze to the world beyond, we see a horizon transformed by the concept of strengths-based teams, leaders, and organizations. This shift in mindset isn't merely a trend but a revolution—reshaping the landscape of workplaces worldwide.

Adoption of the strengths-based approach represents a paradigm shift in work culture across the globe. Traditionally, organizations have been largely problem-focused, emphasizing areas of weakness and improvement. The strengths-based revolution alters this narrative, giving rise to cultures that focus on and nurture inherent strengths. It makes more sense, when we really think about it. The result is an atmosphere of positivity and high morale, where employees feel seen, understood, and valued for their unique contributions.

The impact of this revolution extends beyond individual organizations, infiltrating entire societies and economies. As organizations thrive, job satisfaction increases. As employee engagement rises, productivity and innovation magnify. This positively impacts economic growth. And with employees being more engaged and happier at work, there's an improvement in the quality of life, leading to healthier, happier societies. Locally. Nationally. Globally.

In our rapidly changing world, resilience is crucial for organizational survival and success. By focusing on strengths, organizations build a resilient workforce that adapts to changes swiftly and effectively. Strengths-based organizations harness the diverse strengths of their team members to navigate challenges, and they leverage various perspectives to find innovative solutions. This resilience is especially valuable in times of crisis, as it allows organizations to recover faster and emerge stronger.

In an era of the "Great Resignation," attracting and retaining top talent is a significant challenge for organizations. A strengths-based culture, with its focus on individual growth and recognition, proves to be a powerful magnet for talent. People are naturally drawn to workplaces that value their unique abilities and offer growth opportunities based on their strengths. So, organizations that adopt this approach have a competitive edge in the talent market.

In a world where diversity and inclusion are increasingly prioritized, the strengths-based approach emerges as a strong attractive force. By recognizing and appreciating the unique strengths that individuals bring, organizations naturally promote a culture of diversity—respecting and valuing differences and fostering an inclusive environment where everyone feels a sense of belonging.

By promoting well-being, fostering resilience, and enhancing productivity, the strengths-based revolution contributes significantly to sustainable development. It aligns with several United Nations Sustainable Development Goals, such as decent work and economic growth, reduced inequalities, and optimal health and well-being.

As we travel further into the 21st century, the strengths-based revolution continues to gather momentum, with more and more organizations, leaders, and teams awakening to the immense potential that redounds with focusing on strengths. However, as with any revolution, this requires proactive intent. It's time to future-proof your business and join the strengths-based revolution, so let's explore how you can do that.

Future-Proofing Your Business

The economic landscape forever morphs and shifts. Businesses rise and fall. Industries evolve. Yet, the question remains: How can you future-proof your business amid the perpetual flux? The answer lies within your organization, embedded in the unique strengths of your people. The strengths-based approach is a resilient strategy with profound implications for the future of work and organizational success.

What gives the strengths-based approach its longevity is its emphasis on human development—the *value* of human development. The most forward-thinking organizations no longer view their people as resources, but rather as partners in a journey toward success. This shift in thinking and terminology—from "Human Resources" to "People and Culture"—is fueled by a growing recognition that employees aren't just resources to be managed; they're unique individuals with diverse backgrounds, talents, and experiences.

By focusing on "People and Culture," an organization emphasizes the human side of the workforce. It prioritizes individual well-being and fosters an inclusive culture that values diversity—a more holistic, employee-centric approach. It understands that when people are celebrated and cultures are nurtured, the entire organization flourishes.

The strengths-based approach also fosters adaptability. It's a crucial trait for businesses navigating the complex, fluid landscape of today's global economy. When individuals understand their unique strengths, they leverage them effectively to adapt to changing circumstances. In the face of new challenges or opportunities, a strengths-based team can respond swiftly and effectively. It can reconfigure their collective strengths to meet the new demands—whatever they may be.

As we peer into the future, it's clear that technology, automation, and artificial intelligence will continue to transform the workplace.

Ever more tasks that are currently performed by humans will undoubtedly be automated, but there are aspects of human contribution that machines thankfully can't replicate, including creativity, critical thinking, emotional intelligence, leadership, and personal charisma.

In the face of the AI automation boom, the strengths-based approach offers a way to distinguish the unique human contributions that each team member brings to the table. By focusing on these inherent strengths, businesses leverage the irreplaceable value of their human capital, future-proofing against technological disruption.

The strengths-based approach fosters a culture of continuous learning and innovation. By focusing on strengths, employees are more engaged and motivated, leading to a higher likelihood of innovative thinking and action. This culture of continuous learning and innovation is essential for staying relevant and competitive in the future business landscape.

Finally, the strengths-based approach is essential for fulfilling the promise of diversity and inclusion in the workplace. As organizations seek this greater diversity and inclusivity, recognizing and valuing individual strengths becomes more critical. The strengths-based approach inherently values diversity, acknowledging that everyone has unique strengths to contribute. This is instrumental in creating an inclusive work culture where everyone feels valued and accepted.

As we step boldly into the future, it's clear that the strengths-based approach provides a robust framework for future-proofing your business by capitalizing on the unique strengths of your team. It's not just about surviving in the future; it's also about thriving amid whatever changes come our way.

Action Steps—Your Personal Roadmap

Creating a strengths-based future for your organization may seem like a significant undertaking, but the process can be demystified with a series of actionable steps. This roadmap isn't intended to be a rigid formula, but rather a guide that offers direction while encouraging adaptability and creativity based on your unique circumstances.

Here are some essential steps to shape your strengths-based future:

1. **Develop strengths awareness.** The journey begins with an understanding and appreciation of the concept of strengths. This means recognizing that each person has a unique set of innate talents and abilities that can be nurtured into strengths. Invest time and resources into educating yourself and your organization about the power and potential of a strengths-based approach. This may mean attending workshops and seminars, or engaging a strengths-based coach or consultant.

2. **Identify individual strengths.** Focus on identifying the strengths within your team. As we've pointed out, there are several strengths identification tools available, such as CliftonStrengths, StandOut, VIA Character Strengths, and Strengths Profile. Encourage open discussion about strengths within your team and ensure that every member can discover their individual strengths. The intent is not to label but rather to explore and understand each person's unique talents better. When we understand our colleagues, we appreciate them. When we appreciate them, we value who they are. And when we value them, we put our heads together and leverage our strengths as a team.

3. **Foster a strengths-based culture.** With a shared understanding of strengths, you can start to foster a strengths-based culture within your organization, recognizing and

valuing strengths at every level. Celebrate individual and team successes that arise from leveraging strengths. Encourage people to use their strengths in daily tasks and challenges. Ensure that every team member feels recognized and appreciated for their unique contributions.

4. **Develop strengths-based leaders.** Strengths-based leadership is crucial for sustaining a strengths-based culture. Invest in leadership development that focuses on identifying and leveraging individual strengths. Encourage leaders to adopt a coaching mindset and focus on nurturing the strengths within their teams rather than managing weaknesses. It's not about ignoring weaknesses, but rather about leveraging strengths to manage and minimize the impact of those weaknesses.

5. **Continual learning and development.** A strengths-based approach isn't a one-off intervention; it's an ongoing journey. Continue to invest in learning and development programs that focus on nurturing strengths. As individuals grow and change, their strengths usually evolve, so regular check-ins and refreshers are vital. Cultivate an environment that encourages continuous learning, innovation, and growth.

6. **Measure impact.** Finally, ensure that you have instituted measures to evaluate the impact of your strengths-based approach. This can include employee engagement surveys, performance metrics, and feedback from customers or clients. By assessing the impact of your strengths-based interventions, you continually refine your approach and build on your successes.

Embarking on a strengths-based future requires commitment, effort, and patience. It may involve challenging some deeply held beliefs and changing established ways of working. However, the rewards—a highly engaged, productive team and a thriving, resilient organization—are well worth it.

The strengths-based approach is more than just a strategy; it's a philosophy that values and celebrates the unique contributions of every individual. It's about a work culture where everyone can be their best selves and can contribute their unique strengths to the collective success of the team and the organization. That's the true power of a strengths-based future.

Team Discussion Questions

1. How do you perceive the strengths-based approach impacting the overall health and productivity of a team or organization? Can you share an example from your experience?

2. Reflecting on the idea of a "strengths-based revolution," how do you see this paradigm shift impacting not just our workplaces but our society and economy at large?

3. How can we make sure we're leveraging our team members' unique strengths to foster resilience and adaptability in our organization, especially in times of crisis?

4. How does a strengths-based approach help organizations in attracting and retaining top talent, especially in the era of the "Great Resignation?" Can we implement this in our current hiring and retention strategies?

5. We discuss how the strengths-based approach can help future-proof organizations against technological disruption. What kind of human strengths do you think are irreplaceable, even with the advent of AI and automation?

6. How can we foster a culture of continuous learning and innovation in our organization by leveraging the strengths-based approach? Can we draw on examples from other organizations or our own past experiences?

7. We outline several steps toward creating a strengths-based future, including strengths awareness, identification, culture creation, leadership, continual learning, and impact measurement. How could our organization practically implement each of these steps? Where might we encounter challenges, and how might we overcome them?

9.
The Strengths Journey: A Never-Ending Adventure

Our journey on the strengths canvas is like an artist's masterpiece. It's constantly evolving with each brush stroke—an adventure that celebrates the vibrant colors of our diversity, resilience, and continuous growth.

Painting a Vibrant Future

As we reach the final leg of our journey through the strengths-based landscape, it's essential to underscore that we're on a never-ending adventure—not an expedition with a finite ending or where a box is checked and then forgotten. It's an ongoing discovery. Or perhaps we might call it an evolving masterpiece—like an artist's evolving canvas. Let's call it the "strengths canvas." As we paint our vibrant future, each brush stroke represents the continuous learning and growth that forms the very essence of a strengths-based approach. So then, what might this strengths canvas look like?

On the palette of our strengths canvas are the unique strengths of everyone in our organization. We have the rich and vivid colors that bring life to the canvas. Like the diverse hues on the artist's palette, the unique strengths within your team provide the variety necessary for creating a detailed and captivating masterpiece—with which we can paint an organization that's diverse yet united, dynamic yet harmonious. It's a team replete with creativity and innovation.

Artists often use a technique called layering—applying multiple layers of paint to add depth, color and texture to their artwork.

On our strengths canvas, layering represents the continual development of our strengths. Each layer signifies new experiences and challenges, signifying learning that contributes to the growth and enhancement of our strengths. A never-ending process. Every challenge we face and every success we celebrate adds another layer to our strengths canvas—making us more resilient and vibrant.

Painting a masterpiece takes patience and delicacy. It takes time and dedication. It requires an understanding of the nuances of color and technique—all of which are critical for cultivating a strengths-based organization. It's a mindful, deliberate process that requires us to understand and appreciate the subtle intricacies of everyone's strengths. It involves cultivating an environment where these strengths can be nurtured and expressed fully. It's a culture where every stroke adds value to our workplace artwork.

And, of course, a masterpiece mustn't be hidden away. Rather, we display it for all to see and appreciate. Consequently, a strengths-based organization isn't just about inward growth; it's also about showcasing our strengths to the world. It invites admiration for the unique and powerful contributions that each individual makes. It sets an example for others and inspires them to set out on their own strengths journey.

As we embark on this exciting journey, we must remember that painting our strengths canvas isn't about creating a perfect picture; it's about embracing the beauty of diversity. Embark. Embrace. It's fostering the thrill of continuous growth and the power of individual strengths and architecting an organization where every stroke counts—and every color shines brightly. This is the vibrant and dynamic future we envision with a strengths-based approach.

Just like an artist stepping back to admire their masterpiece, we too look upon our strengths canvas with pride. It represents a collective effort where every individual has contributed their unique strengths. Each stroke of the brush has a story to tell and a lesson to impart. Our strengths canvas is a living, breathing testament to the power of strengths, and it's an adventure that continues to evolve, surprise, and inspire. That's the beauty of the strengths journey—a never-ending and harmonious adventure.

The Strengths Trek

Like all exciting treks, the strengths journey is *about* the journey. It's not necessarily a final destination. Instead, it's primarily about the experiences and relationships we have along the way. It's about the growth we witness within ourselves and others, and about the transformation that occurs in our teams and organizations. This journey, embarked upon with the spirit of discovery and understanding, explores the vast landscape of our strengths and potential. Let's call it the "strengths trek"—an expedition that takes us to never-imagined heights, forging paths that lead to astounding results and success, unlocking the power of human magic that resides within us.

The strengths trek begins with the decision to embrace a new perspective—to view individuals, teams, and organizations through the lens of strengths. It's a commitment to seek and to recognize the unique gifts within each of us, with a goal to honor these human gifts by giving them room to shine. Embarking on this journey requires courage to step away from the conventional focus on weaknesses, and instead to celebrate and amplify what's right and powerful within us. An ancient sage said it well: "The glory of God is a human being fully alive."[10] Indeed, honoring and cultivating strengths certainly does make a person fully alive.

Once we've decided to undertake our journey, the next step is mapping our path, which involves the identification and understanding of everyone's strengths. What are the unique skills, talents, and abilities that they bring to the table? How can these be leveraged

---

[10] This quote is attributed to St. Irenaeus, a Christian theologian and bishop of Lyons in the 2nd century AD.

for maximum impact? These answers form the roadmap for our journey, guiding our steps toward an environment that's energized, productive, and full of potential.

The landscape of the strengths trek is diverse and dynamic. It consists of various terrains, each representing a different prospect of a strengths-based approach. There are valleys representing the depth of our untapped potential. There are mountains symbolizing the peaks of achievement we can reach by leveraging our strengths. And there are rivers reflecting the flow of creativity and innovation that spring from a strengths-based mindset. Trekking through this landscape is an exhilarating experience, filled with discovery, growth, and transformation.

The exciting and ongoing strengths trek journey requires consistent effort and commitment. Sustaining it involves nurturing an environment that encourages continuous learning and growth. It's about fostering a culture that values and celebrates individual strengths, creating a sense of belonging and engagement among team members. This culture becomes the fuel that powers the journey. It's the accelerant that catalyzes teams and organizations into powerhouses of productivity, innovation, and success.

And all of this is, of course, a shared trek. Celebrate your successes. Learn from challenges. Inspire one another to reach greater heights. This collective experience not only fosters a sense of camaraderie but also strengthens the bonds within teams, enhancing collaboration and synergy.

As we traverse the landscape of our strengths trek, we must continually remind ourselves that the journey is as important as the destination. It's a trek that encourages exploration, celebrates diversity, and values the unique contributions of everyone, welcoming continuous growth as a natural part of our journey. It's an exciting adventure that transforms teams and organizations, empowering them to scale new heights of success.

And it continues to inspire, surprise, and enlighten us. Every step we take on this journey brings us closer to a future that values strengths, promotes growth, and celebrates success. With each passing milestone, we gain a deeper understanding of our strengths and how they can drive us toward excellence. And as we continue on this trek, we're not just charting a course for our growth, but we're also paving the way for a more engaged, productive, and vibrant future.

The strengths trek is a journey of continuous growth, discovery, and transformation.

Team Discussion Questions

1. How can recognizing and harnessing our individual strengths lead to a "positive revolution" in our workplace? Can you share some examples from your own experiences?

2. What does the strengths-canvas metaphor mean to you? How does it apply to our team and organization?

3. In our team, how can we better use the "layering" technique, where we use our experiences and challenges to develop and enhance our strengths?

4. How can we nurture an environment that allows the unique strengths of each team member to be fully expressed and appreciated?

5. We explored the concept of the strengths trek as primarily an adventure, not a destination. How does this concept resonate with you in your personal and professional journey?

6. Considering the strengths trek, how can we better map our individual and team strengths to maximize impact and productivity in our organization?

7. The strengths trek suggests the importance of sharing the journey and learning from challenges collectively. How can we better celebrate successes, learn from challenges, and inspire each other in our team?

Resources for Managers and Teams

25 Strengths-Based Interview Questions

1. Can you tell me about a time when you used your top strengths to solve a challenging situation at work?

2. Which of your skills or talents are you most proud of, and how have they been beneficial in your previous roles?

3. What would your former colleagues say is your most valuable strength?

4. How have you used your unique strengths to contribute to a team?

5. Can you share an instance where your strengths helped you to overcome a project obstacle?

6. Which of your skills or strengths do you think are most relevant to this position?

7. How do your strengths align with our company values and culture?

8. Can you describe a time when you were able to capitalize on a coworker's strengths?

9. How do you manage or compensate for your weaknesses in the workplace?

10. Tell me about a project or accomplishment that you consider to be the most significant in your career.

11. How have you used feedback to improve your skills or capitalize on your strengths?

12. Can you describe a situation when one of your strengths was crucial in dealing with a difficult client or coworker?

13. Tell me about a time when you had to leverage your strengths to learn a new skill or technology quickly.

14. In your experience, how has your understanding of your strengths and weaknesses helped you professionally?

15. How do you think this job will allow you to utilize your strengths?

16. Can you share an example of how you've helped a team member to identify or utilize their strengths?

17. How have you used your strengths to handle a high-pressure situation?

18. How have you navigated a situation where a role did not play to your strengths?

19. Tell me about a time when your strengths helped you to drive change or innovation.

20. Can you describe a situation when your strengths enabled you to exceed expectations on a task or project?

21. How would leveraging your strengths make a difference to our team or organization?

22. Can you tell me about a time when your strengths directly influenced your career path or decisions?

23. Tell me about a time when you took on a task that was outside your usual responsibilities and how your strengths played a part.

24. Have you ever had to use your strengths to make a difficult decision? How did that go?

25. Can you describe how your top strengths will help you to succeed in this role?

25 Ideas for Strengths-Based Employee Feedback

1. Identify specific examples of when the employee used their strengths effectively in their role.

2. Highlight how their strengths have contributed positively to the team's dynamics or goals.

3. Suggest new opportunities or projects where their strengths could be put to great use.

4. Compliment their ability to use their strengths creatively and innovatively.

5. Connect their strengths to their past accomplishments and contributions to the company.

6. Show them how their strengths align with the company's vision or objectives.

7. Discuss ways they can further develop and utilize their strengths in their current role.

8. Provide constructive feedback on how they can better leverage their strengths in challenging situations.

9. Encourage them to take on leadership roles or responsibilities that align with their strengths.

10. Commend their use of strengths to overcome difficult situations or obstacles.

11. Suggest training or professional development opportunities that align with their strengths.

12. Highlight instances where their utilization of strengths helped team members.

13. Discuss their progress in roles or tasks that require the use of their strengths.

14. Encourage them to mentor others in the areas where they're strong.

15. Acknowledge their self-awareness and management of their weaknesses while also capitalizing on their strengths.

16. Provide positive reinforcement when they step outside of their comfort zone but still play to their strengths.

17. Identify when their strengths have positively impacted client or customer relationships.

18. Praise their ability to balance the use of their strengths and team collaboration.

19. Recognize their effort to use their strengths to learn and adapt to new processes or technologies.

20. Discuss how their strengths could play a part in their career growth within the company.

21. Celebrate their use of strengths to achieve individual or team targets.

22. Highlight how their strengths have improved the overall performance of the team.

23. Praise their initiative in using their strengths to solve problems.

24. Point out occasions when they've transferred their strengths to new or unfamiliar tasks.

25. Discuss how their unique strengths contribute to the diversity and richness of the team.

25 Ideas for Strengths-Based Performance Reviews

1. Discuss specific instances where the employee has utilized their strengths to achieve goals and objectives.

2. Highlight the positive impact of the employee's strengths on their work, their team, and the company.

3. Evaluate how the employee has developed and harnessed their strengths over the review period.

4. Provide examples of when the employee has used their strengths to overcome challenges or solve complex problems.

5. Acknowledge the employee's ability to leverage their strengths to drive innovation or improvement.

6. Discuss how the employee's strengths align with the values and objectives of the company.

7. Highlight times when the employee's strengths contributed to team cohesion or morale.

8. Identify opportunities where the employee's strengths can be better utilized or further developed.

9. Reflect on the progress the employee has made in their role while using their strengths.

10. Encourage the employee to take on new responsibilities or challenges that align with their strengths.

11. Acknowledge the positive impact of the employee's strengths on customer or client relationships.

12. Suggest areas of professional development that align with the employee's strengths.

13. Discuss how the employee's strengths have contributed to their personal growth and development.

14. Note the employee's ability to balance their strengths with the strengths of others in the team.

15. Highlight how the employee has used their strengths to adapt to changes or new technologies.

16. Encourage the employee to mentor or share their strengths with others in the team.

17. Recognize how the employee's strengths have played a role in the achievement of team or company targets.

18. Discuss the unique value the employee's strengths brings to their role and the team.

19. Provide constructive feedback on how the employee can better manage or utilize their strengths.

20. Celebrate the employee's initiative in using their strengths to contribute positively to the workplace.

21. Reflect on the employee's use of their strengths in collaboration and team projects.

22. Highlight the employee's resilience and ability to use their strengths in stressful or challenging situations.

23. Discuss how the employee's strengths can play a part in their future career growth within the company.

24. Suggest ways the employee can further cultivate their strengths outside of their current role.

25. Close with a summary of the employee's strengths and their positive impact on the company.

Facilitating One-on-One Employee Strengths Debriefs

The strengths assessment is a powerful tool for revealing an employee's unique talents and capabilities. It offers deep insights into individual preferences, natural abilities, and potential areas of growth. The assessment should be taken as only the first step in understanding full potential. As a manager, your role is crucial in helping employees to understand, interpret, and apply their results in the workplace.

One of the most effective ways to do this is by conducting a one-on-one debrief with each team member. These sessions offer an opportunity to discuss the employee's strengths in detail, providing a space for open dialogue about their unique abilities and how they can be best utilized within the team.

The questions listed below are designed to facilitate a meaningful conversation about the employee's strengths results. They encourage reflection on the results and invite employees to consider how their strengths manifest in their daily tasks. The questions also stimulate discussion about how these strengths can be further developed and leveraged for team success.

Using these questions as a guide, you can help your employees to better understand their strengths, recognize the value they bring to the team, and develop a plan to integrate these strengths more effectively into their work. This process can also help to boost their engagement, increase productivity, and foster a positive and strengths-focused team culture.

The goal isn't just to discuss the results but to create an action plan that enables your employees to apply their strengths in their role, leading to greater job satisfaction and better team performance. Before you embark on these one-on-one sessions, prepare yourself to listen, encourage, and guide your employees in their strengths-based development journey.

Leading a One-on-One Strengths Debrief

Here are 15 questions to use in a one-on-one managerial debrief session:

1. **Can you share your top strengths as highlighted in your assessment?**

   Allows you to understand their key strengths as perceived by their assessment. Sets the foundation for the conversation.

2. **Was there any element in your top strengths that caught you off guard?**

   Gives you insight into their self-perception and how it aligns or differs from the assessment.

3. **Which one of your top strengths resonates with you the most, and can you explain why?**

   Helps you to identify the strengths they identify with strongly and are likely to leverage naturally in their work.

4. **What fresh perspectives about yourself did you gain after going through your strengths?**

   Provides a window into their self-awareness, as well as their openness to learning and growth.

5. **Among your numerous strengths, can you identify two that you believe you execute exceptionally well?**

   Helps you to understand where they believe their strongest abilities lie, which can be useful in task assignment and team role designation.

6. **What complimentary phrases do people who know you well typically use to characterize you?**

   Gives you an external view of their strengths and their impact on those around them.

7. **Can you describe the aspects of your current position that you find most fulfilling?**

   Helps to identify what tasks and responsibilities align most closely with their strengths and increase their job satisfaction.

8. **Recall a day at work that you felt was exceptional. What made it stand out? What did you achieve?**

   Reveals what kind of tasks, interactions, and achievements they find particularly motivating.

9. **What do you feel is your distinct value-add to our team?**

   Helps them to articulate their unique contribution and makes them feel valued and appreciated.

10. **Which among your identified strengths do you think contributes the most to our team's success?**

    Provides insight into how they perceive their role within the team, as well as their impact on team performance.

11. **How can I assist you in leveraging your strengths more effectively in your role?**

    Offers them an opportunity to voice their needs and expectations from you as their manager, promoting open communication.

12. **Are there any responsibilities or aspects of your job that you'd like to engage in more often?**

    Gives you an understanding of their aspirations and what aspects of work they're most drawn to.

13. **Considering your strengths report, what should I understand about collaborating with you?**

    Gives you insight into how they prefer to be managed and collaborated with, aiding in nurturing effective working relationships.

14. **How do your top strengths add merit to our team's dynamics and performance?**

    Offers a clear perspective on how they see their strengths influencing team dynamics and outcomes.

15. **How do these talents aid you in successfully accomplishing your assigned tasks?**

    Helps you to understand how they leverage their strengths in their role, providing insight into their approach to work.

Manager's Next Steps

After the comprehensive debrief, you'll find yourself loaded with a treasure trove of information about your employee's strengths, ambitions, and preferred work styles. To maximize the potential of this newfound knowledge, here are some steps to consider:

1. **Reflect on the discussion.** Spend time digesting the information you gathered during the debrief. Look for emerging patterns and insights that'll help you to gain a deeper understanding of your employee and how to best employ their strengths.

2. **Assess strengths alignment with their current role.** Evaluate whether the strengths your employee identified align with their current duties. If there's a misalignment, you might need to modify their job design or the way the job is executed, so they can use their natural talents more frequently.

3. **Develop an action plan.** Drawing from the insights, formulate a personalized development plan for your employee, which should focus on ways they can leverage their strengths to improve their performance and job engagement. It should also focus on potential opportunities for them to use their strengths in novel ways.

4. **Share feedback and plan.** Communicate your insights and action plan to your employee. Make sure they understand and agree with the proposed steps. This fosters a sense of transparency and commitment from them.

5. **Promote strengths-based collaboration.** Create a culture where employees are encouraged to utilize each other's strengths. Enlighten team members about others' strengths (with their approval) and motivate them to account for these when it comes to team tasks.

6. **Enact changes.** If your debrief pointed toward a job redesign or suggested new projects that allow your employee to apply their strengths, you should start working on implementing these changes. This might involve discussing options with senior management, HR, or People and Culture.

7. **Carry out regular follow-ups.** Periodic check-ins following the debrief are crucial to ensure that the plan is effective and that the employee feels more engaged and satisfied. Adjust the plan based on these follow-up meetings when necessary.

Your objective here is to create an atmosphere where employees feel valued and driven to contribute to the team's success using their strengths. Your role as a manager is to guide, support, and offer opportunities for this to occur.

Frequently Asked Questions: Strengths-Based Teams and Organizations

The Difference Between Employee Strengths and Skills

When it comes to human resources and people development, the terms "strengths" and "skills" are often used interchangeably, but they're not the same. Understanding the difference between the two is crucial for managers who aim to leverage the full potential of their team members and create an engaged, effective workforce.

"Skills"—properly speaking—refers to the learned abilities or expertise that an individual has gained through training, education, and experience. They're typically task-oriented, specific, and transferable between jobs or sectors. For instance, a skill could be proficiency in a foreign language, the ability to code in a specific programming language, or the capacity to create a project plan using a project management tool. Skills can be measured and assessed objectively, and they're often listed as qualifications on job postings and resumes.

Conversely, "strengths" refers to the inherent qualities or attributes that an individual possesses and demonstrates naturally. They're the unique combination of talents, knowledge, and skills that an individual uses consistently to achieve success. Strengths are less about what you *do* and more about what you *are*—an alchemy of talent (who you are) and skills. Strengths encompass a person's character and personality traits. Using strengths gives a person energy.

An example of a strength would be strategic thinking, empathy, resilience, positivity, creativity, or adaptability. For instance, a team member may be particularly *skilled* at financial analysis, but the way they approach problems with a detail-oriented, analytical mindset may be a natural *strength*. Another employee might have exceptional skills in public speaking, but their natural ability to empathize and connect with people makes their oral presentations more engaging and effective. This would be a strength—enhancing a skill.

So, skills are often acquired and developed over time, while strengths are more inherent—and can be nurtured and refined, as they represent a person's natural inclinations and talents. And while skills contribute to task completion, strengths often dictate the approach an individual will take to problem-solving and the way they interact with others.

As a manager, understanding this difference can be quite beneficial—allowing you to assign tasks more effectively, helping you to foster a positive working environment, as well as encouraging personal and professional development among team members. By focusing on strengths, you're not just considering what your employees can do, but you're also considering how they can do those things in the most effective, efficient, and satisfying way. This significantly improves motivation, boosting productivity and cultivating job satisfaction. And, of course, it leads to better results for the individual, the team, and the organization.

The Difference Between Talent and Strength

The terms "talent" and "strength" are also often used interchangeably, but there's a distinct difference in the context of personal development and performance management. Understanding the difference is crucial for effective management and employee development.

"Talent" refers to an individual's natural aptitude or innate ability. It's inherent within all of us—an inborn pattern of thought, feeling, or behavior that can be productively applied.[11] These are often the activities or behaviors we engage in instinctively and find innately satisfying. For example, a person may have a talent for music (with a good ear for rhythm and melody), or they may have a talent for leadership (naturally excelling at motivating and directing others).

"Strength," however, is an admixture of talent and performance in a specific activity; it's often a refined talent, honed and developed over time. So, strengths have the addition of skills and knowledge, being the product of talent that's been cultivated through learning and practice.

For instance, you may have a natural talent for drawing, with an eye for detail and the ability to sketch with ease. Your talent becomes a strength when you've honed and developed it—after you study art and learn different techniques, when you practice regularly and gain knowledge about different materials and styles. Once this talent is honed into a strength, you consistently create high-quality art. *Now* it's your strength.

So talent is an innate ability, while strength is developed talent. But while every strength is rooted in talent, not every talent necessarily becomes a strength. It must first be nurtured, developed, and used productively.

As a manager, understanding the distinction between talent and strength allows you to identify the inherent abilities of your team members and aids you in helping them to develop their talents into strengths. This clear focus leads to increased employee engagement, job satisfaction, and productivity, benefitting the individual, the team, and the organization.

---

[11] Gallup, Inc. "StrengthsFinder 2.0." Gallup's Strengths Center, 2007.

Managers Use Strengths to Better Lead Teams

Understanding and leveraging their strengths is critical for any manager aspiring to lead effectively, allowing them to inspire trust, drive engagement, garner a positive work environment, and empower their team to excel. Let's look at an example of how a manager can use their individual strengths to lead their team more effectively.

Sophia, a manager, has strengths in strategic thinking, empathy, and communication. Here's how she might use these strengths to lead her team:

1. **Strategic thinking.** With her strength in strategic thinking, Sophia easily sees patterns, anticipates future scenarios, and devises effective solutions for complex problems. She uses this strength to guide her team, helping them to prioritize tasks and navigate challenges to align with the broader business goals. By sharing her vision and strategic plans with the team, she keeps everyone focused and engaged.

2. **Empathy.** Her strength in empathy allows her to understand and share the feelings of her team members and build strong relationships with them. She naturally fosters a culture of trust and openness. By empathizing with her team's challenges and stresses, Sophia provides tailored support and encouragement, helping them to overcome obstacles and maintain morale.

3. **Communication.** As a strong communicator, she expresses her ideas clearly and persuasively, using this strength to ensure that her team understands their roles, expectations, and the reasons behind decisions. Her open and transparent communication builds trust, minimizing misunderstanding and keeping everyone on the same page.

To leverage these strengths effectively, Sophia must be aware of her strengths and consciously apply them in her leadership role. For instance, she might plan regular team meetings to share insights (strategic thinking), or conduct one-on-one check-ins with her team members to understand their feelings and perspectives (empathy). This ensures that she conveys decisions and updates clearly and consistently (communication).

But Sophia must also be mindful of the potential downsides of overusing her strengths. For example, too much strategic thinking without action can lead to analysis paralysis. Excessive empathy can lead to emotional burnout, and over-communication can result in information overload. Balancing the use of strengths with the recognition (and use of) the strengths of others on her team is key to effective leadership.

This balanced use of strengths allows Sophia to create an environment where her team feels understood, motivated, and aligned toward common goals, leading to higher team performance, job satisfaction, and retention.

Addressing Skeptical Resistance

Creating a strengths-based culture in a team can often be met with resistance. Some team members may view it as a diversion from regular work or even a waste of time. Below are a few ways to get your team to buy into a strengths-based culture:

1. **Communicate the benefits.** Clearly explain the advantages of a strengths-based culture, communicating how it increases engagement, productivity, and satisfaction. Share data or case studies from other organizations that've successfully implemented a strengths-based approach. For example, you could say, "According to a Gallup study, teams that focus on their strengths are 8.9% more profitable, and individuals who use their strengths every day are six times

more likely to be engaged at work. This isn't just about feeling good; it's about achieving our strategic objectives more effectively."

2. **Start small.** Introduce the strengths-based approach gradually. Start with a pilot project or a small team, and then let the results speak for themselves. For instance, you might initiate a "Strengths Spotlight" during team meetings, where each week a different team member shares their top strengths. Have them share how they've used them effectively. Over time, this highlights the real-world impact of leveraging strengths.

3. **Provide training.** Offer workshops or training sessions to help your team understand what strengths are, how to identify their own, and how to utilize them in daily work. For example, you might bring in a strengths-based coach for a workshop, or use tools like CliftonStrengths to help your team discover and understand their unique strengths.

4. **Lead by example.** Show your commitment to a strengths-based culture by openly discussing your own strengths. Explain how you're using them in your leadership role. You might say, "One of my key strengths is strategic thinking, and I've used this to develop our new project plan. I'd like to pair this with someone's strength in execution to really make this project successful."

5. **Embed it into processes.** Incorporate strengths-based discussions into regular team meetings, performance reviews, and project-planning sessions. This demonstrates that it's not an add-on, but rather an integral part of how the team operates. For instance, during performance reviews, instead of solely focusing on areas of improvement, spend significant time discussing how the individual can leverage and develop their existing strengths.

6. **Acknowledge success.** When you see team members using their strengths effectively, acknowledge and celebrate it. This validates the individual's effort and shows the team the positive outcomes of a strengths-based approach. If a team member uses their "Positivity" strength to keep the team morale high during a challenging project, make a point of recognizing their contribution. Communicate its impact on the team's success.

A strengths-based culture isn't about ignoring weaknesses; it's about helping everyone to realize that focusing on and developing their strengths leads to higher performance, better results, and a more satisfying work experience. If your goal is to not fail, focus on weakness fixing. But if your goal is to thrive, focus on accelerating strengths and managing weakness.

Use Strengths to Tackle Tasks and Meet Goals

Using your strengths to accomplish challenging goals and tasks often involves creative application and adaptation of existing abilities. Here are a few strategies and examples:

1. **Complementary application.** Use your strengths to complement the task at hand. For example, if you're an excellent communicator but struggle with data analysis, you might utilize your communication skills to reach out to colleagues or experts who can help explain complex data concepts to you, or facilitate a collaborative analysis session where you and others can tackle the data together.

2. **Strengths pairing.** Pair your strengths with the difficult task to create a better approach. If you have a strength in creativity but are struggling with a mundane administrative task, find ways to make the task more engaging. Perhaps you could develop a unique filing system, or create a

visually stimulating spreadsheet that makes the data more appealing to work with.

3. **Learning through strengths.** Use your strengths as a learning tool. If you have a strength in curiosity and love learning new things but are faced with a challenging task that you don't have much knowledge about, try to perceive it as an opportunity to satisfy your curiosity and learn something new.

4. **Strengths as motivation.** Your strengths can also serve as the impetus to getting things done. If you have a strength in achievement and you're faced with a difficult project, frame the completion of the project as a significant accomplishment. The satisfaction you derive from completing a challenging task serves as motivation to push through the difficulty.

5. **Delegating.** If you're able to do so, delegate tasks in which you have a weakness to others who possess strengths in those areas and then offer your own strengths to support their work. For example, if you're a strategic thinker but weak in detail-oriented tasks, delegate detailed work to a team member who excels in this area. You can then use your strategic thinking to map out the bigger picture and guide the overall direction.

Everyone has areas of strength. By leveraging your strengths creatively, you can effectively navigate through these challenging tasks. The key lies in recognizing your strengths and knowing how to apply them to different situations.

A Culture That Attracts and Retains Talent

Creating a strengths-based culture can work wonders in attracting and retaining top talent in your organization. Here's how:

1. **Making your organization attractive.** A strengths-based culture signals to prospective employees that your organization values individuality and personal development. When prospective personnel realize they'll be valued for their unique strengths and not just their technical skills, your organization becomes much more attractive.

2. **Boosting morale and engagement.** When you recognize and appreciate your employees for their unique strengths, they feel more satisfied and engaged in their work. Higher engagement often results in increased productivity and innovation, which further enhances your organization's reputation.

3. **Fostering professional growth.** A strengths-based culture encourages continuous learning and growth. By focusing on strengths, you create an environment where employees continuously develop and apply their strengths in new and exciting ways. This fosters a culture of professional growth, making employees feel more connected to their work and less likely to look for opportunities elsewhere.

4. **Building strong teams.** When employees understand their strengths and their colleagues' strengths, they collaborate more effectively. This leads to more effective, cohesive teams, boosts overall organizational performance, and increases employee satisfaction and retention.

5. **Enhancing employee well-being.** Focusing on strengths rather than weaknesses also has a positive impact on employees' psychological well-being. Employees who use their strengths regularly are more likely to be happier, more confident, and less stressed. This contributes to lower turnover rates.

6. **Encouraging openness and transparency.** In a strengths-based culture, employees are encouraged to be open about

their strengths and areas for development. This fosters a culture of transparency and mutual respect, as well as helping to reduce conflict, improve teamwork, and ultimately, increase staff retention.

By building a strengths-based culture, you're not just fostering an environment where people are happier and more productive; you're also creating a workplace that attracts and retains the best talent. If you are genuine and consistent in your approach, you ensure that a focus on strengths permeates every aspect of your organization.

Breaking Down Silos

Silos—isolated departments within an organization—often hamper communication, inhibit collaboration, and stunt overall growth. Building a strengths-based culture is a game changer in breaking down these silos. Here's how:

1. **Fostering understanding and respect.** By focusing on individual strengths, people across different departments begin to understand and appreciate the unique contributions each person brings to the table, resulting in a broad sense of respect and understanding across an organization.

2. **Promoting cross-functional collaboration.** A strengths-based approach encourages people to seek out others with complementary strengths to achieve their goals. As people recognize the value of diverse strengths and perspectives, it leads to more cross-departmental collaboration.

3. **Enhancing communication.** In a strengths-based culture, open communication is essential. As you and your colleagues discuss individual strengths, you're likely to find that you're having broader conversations about goals, challenges, and working together. This openness helps to improve communication between departments.

4. **Encouraging knowledge sharing.** When individuals understand their strengths, they're often more confident and willing to share expertise. This willingness to share knowledge can permeate across departmental boundaries, helping to break down the barriers that silos create.

5. **Creating a shared language.** A strengths-based approach can create a shared language across your organization. When everyone understands the strengths vocabulary, it's easier to discuss how to best work together, regardless of department or role.

6. **Building a unified culture.** Perhaps most importantly, a strengths-based culture promotes a sense of unity. By recognizing that everyone, no matter their department, contributes valuable strengths, you're fostering a unified, inclusive culture that transcends departmental silos.

A strengths-based culture helps to break down silos by fostering respect, promoting collaboration, enhancing communication, and building a unified culture. Such a culture values the unique strengths everyone brings—regardless of department or role.

A Strengths Focus Boosts Trust and Engagement

Building a strengths-based culture in your organization greatly enhances employee engagement and trust in several ways. Here's how:

1. **Boosting self-esteem and motivation.** When you focus on the unique strengths of your team members, it fosters self-esteem and boosts motivation. They feel valued and appreciated for their unique contribution, leading to higher engagement in their work.

2. **Promoting job satisfaction.** A strengths-based approach allows individuals to do what they enjoy and are naturally

good at. This creates higher job satisfaction, and it's a significant factor in overall employee engagement.

3. **Encouraging open communication.** In a strengths-based culture, open conversations about individual strengths and how they can be leveraged are common. This type of dialogue improves communication within your team, ensuring that employees feel more connected to each other and the organization.

4. **Fostering a sense of belonging.** A strengths-based culture celebrates the diversity of talents within a team, bolstering a sense of belonging. When employees feel like they belong, they're more likely to engage in their work and commit to their team and organization.

5. **Building trust.** Recognizing and valuing each other's strengths leads to greater trust among team members. As you and your team acknowledge and rely on each other's strengths, you're showing that you trust each other's abilities. This trust deepens over time, creating a strong foundation for collaboration and innovation.

6. **Fueling growth and development.** A focus on strengths doesn't just improve performance; it also spurs growth and development. When employees get to use and improve their strengths, they feel more optimistic about their personal growth in the organization, which leads to higher engagement.

By developing a strengths-based culture, you're not just placing a bet on your team's talents; you're also investing in their engagement, their trust in each other, and the success of your organization.

A Strengths Focus Enhances Performance

Building a strengths-based culture in your organization often dramatically accelerates high performance. It can:

1. **Maximize productivity.** When you tap into the natural strengths of your team members, they perform tasks more efficiently and effectively. They're energized and productive when doing what they're innately good at.

2. **Enhance creativity and innovation.** A strengths-based culture encourages diversity of thought by valuing and leveraging everyone's unique strengths, leading to more creative and innovative solutions to challenges.

3. **Improve problem-solving.** When team members use their strengths, they're more equipped to tackle challenges and find solutions. They can apply their unique perspectives and skills to overcome obstacles, enhancing the problem-solving capabilities of your team.

4. **Increase resilience.** When employees feel confident in their strengths, they're more resilient in the face of adversity, knowing that they have the strengths to cope with difficulties. This contributes to the team's overall capacity to adapt to change or recover from setbacks.

5. **Boost team synergy.** A strengths-based culture creates a natural synergy within teams, as each team member brings their unique strengths to the table. When these strengths are well-coordinated, they can complement each other to create a highly efficient team.

6. **Enhance job satisfaction.** Employees who use their strengths regularly are more likely to be satisfied with their jobs, and job satisfaction is a key performance factor. Sat-

isfied employees are more engaged and committed to their work, which results in higher performance levels.

7. **Promote growth and development.** Focusing on strengths can also help with professional development. When employees can build on their strengths, they can expand their skillsets and capabilities. This contributes to the continuous improvement and high performance of your team.

By focusing on strengths, you plumb the untapped potential within your organization, propelling your team toward high performance and setting your organization apart in the competitive business landscape.

Break-Out Activities for Teams

1. Strengths Mapping Activity

Objective: To create a visual representation of the different strengths each team member possesses. To stimulate conversation on how these strengths can be individually and collaboratively used to drive team success.

Materials needed: The strengths assessment results from each team member (e.g., Gallup's CliftonStrengths, StandOut, or VIA Character Strengths), a large whiteboard or poster paper, markers, and sticky notes.

Procedure:

1. Have each team member complete a strengths assessment before the meeting and bring the results with them. For this activity, you'll focus on the top strengths of each individual.

2. Prepare a large grid on the whiteboard or poster paper. Write each team member's name along the top row and list the identified strengths in the first column.

3. As the facilitator, you start the activity by sharing your top strengths. Put a sticky note in each corresponding grid cell and give a brief example of how you've utilized each strength in your work.

4. Each team member then follows suit. They place sticky notes for their top strengths in the corresponding grid cells and share examples of how these strengths have benefited them in their roles.

5. Once everyone's strengths are marked out, take a moment to examine the layout of the strengths on the grid. Prompt a discussion using guiding questions, such as:

   ○ What strengths are most common among the team, and how can these be maximized?

   ○ Which strengths are unique, and how do they bring a different perspective or capability?

   ○ Are there less represented strengths, and what effect might that have on the team?

Outcome: The Strengths Mapping Activity enables your team to visually comprehend the unique composition of strengths within the group. It also helps each person to see how their strengths contribute to the overall abilities of the team, which creates a sense of value and belonging.

It also encourages open discussion about how these strengths can be optimally utilized in teamwork and decision-making. Recognizing the unique and shared strengths within the team informs future task allocation, problem-solving approaches, and even conflict resolution by playing to each member's strengths.

And acknowledging the less-represented strengths steers strategic decisions, such as targeted learning and development or even future hiring, to complement the existing strengths of the team. Your goal is to harness the diversity of strengths to create a more effective, resilient, and engaged team.

2. Strengths Storytelling Activity

Objective: To nurture trust, enhance understanding, and develop a deeper appreciation of everyone's unique strengths by sharing personal narratives.

Materials needed: The strengths assessment results from each team member and a comfortable, circular seating arrangement to facilitate open conversation.

Procedure:

1. Ask each team member to prepare beforehand by recalling a specific scenario where they efficiently employed one of their top strengths in a professional context. The story should be something they're comfortable sharing that vividly demonstrates the strength in action.

2. During the meeting, organize seating in a circle to encourage a sense of equality and openness. Kick off the session by briefly restating the aim of the activity—to improve the understanding, appreciation, and utilization of each other's strengths.

3. As the facilitator, you'll lead by example and share your story first. Discuss the challenge you encountered, the strength you harnessed, and the result. For instance, you might share, "I was handling a project once that was behind schedule, which caused a lot of stress. I utilized my 'Harmony' strength to resolve disagreements within the team. It refocused everyone's attention on our common objective as I proposed a compromise solution. This strategy helped us to get back on track and alleviate tension."

4. Encourage each team member to share their story in turn, ensuring that there's space for questions and reflections after each narration.

5. Once everyone has shared, initiate a discussion. Pose questions such as:

    o   How did it feel to use your strength in that situation?

- ○ How can we create more opportunities to deploy these strengths in our work?

- ○ What new insights do you have about your colleagues' strengths?

Outcome: The Strengths Storytelling Activity enables members to witness each other's strengths in action, thereby understanding their practical application. As individuals share their personal stories, they also divulge a part of their professional identity, which contributes to trust and rapport-building.

This exercise helps team members to appreciate the range of strengths within their team, comprehend how they can supplement each other, and brainstorm ways they can apply their strengths in varied scenarios. The activity nurtures a strengths-based mindset that positively influences collaboration, problem solving, and the general dynamics of your team.

3. Strengths Roleplay Activity

Objective: To deepen your team's understanding of each other's strengths, cultivate empathy, and improve problem-solving using a strengths-based approach through roleplaying scenarios.

Materials needed: The strengths assessment results from each team member, pre-prepared scenario cards, and space for teams to roleplay.

Procedure:

1. Prepare several scenario cards ahead of time. Each card describes a common workplace situation that requires problem solving, decision making, or conflict resolution.

2. Start by dividing your team into groups of 3 to 4 members.

3. Each group then picks a scenario card; they'll roleplay this scenario twice.

4. In the first round, instruct each person to respond to the scenario as they would naturally, using their strengths spontaneously (without thinking about them consciously).

5. After the first round, have the group discuss the dynamics and outcomes. Ask them questions such as:

    o   What strengths did you notice in play?

    o   How did each person's strengths contribute to the outcome of the scenario?

    o   Were any strengths overused or underused?

6. For the second round, ask each group member to consciously use a specific strength from their strengths assessment in the scenario.

7. After the second round, prompt the group to discuss how deliberately using strengths affected the outcome of the scenario. Was it resolved more effectively? Was the communication better?

Example: One of your scenario cards might read, "A team is behind on a project deadline due to miscommunication and conflicting priorities. What steps can you take to resolve the situation?"

In the first round, a team member might naturally apply their "Communication" strength to clear up misunderstandings. Another member might employ their "Responsibility" strength to reprioritize tasks and steer the team toward the deadline.

In the second round, the member who used their "Communication" strength could consciously apply their "Strategic" strength to analyze the situation, identify the core issue, and plan a clear roadmap to complete the project on time.

Outcome: Through the Strengths Roleplay Activity, you're creating a safe space for your team to explore and understand each other's strengths. This exercise promotes empathy, mutual respect, and greater perspective. As they step into each other's shoes, they'll appreciate how different strengths can contribute to a situation.

By roleplaying the same scenario twice, you're showing your team how different strengths can change a situation's outcome, reinforcing the idea that various strengths can contribute to effective problem-solving.

4. Strengths Appreciation Exercise

Objective: To cultivate an environment of mutual recognition and appreciation within your team. This exercise aids in acknowledging the unique strengths of each team member and understanding their contributions to the team's success.

Materials needed: The strengths assessment results from each team member, small slips of paper or sticky notes, and pens.

Procedure:

1. Before beginning, have each team member complete a strengths assessment. If they've already completed one, ask them to bring their results. This forms the basis of the exercise.

2. Start by distributing slips of paper or sticky notes to each member. Ask everyone to write their name on one side of the slip. On the other side, have each person write their top five strengths from the assessment.

3. Collect all the slips in a bowl or a box, then draw one slip at a time. Announce the name and the top strengths of the individual on the slip to the group.

4. Next, open the floor to the rest of the members. Encourage them to share specific instances or examples of when they observed the individual using these strengths in their work. For instance, someone might recall, "I noticed Allie used her 'Adaptability' strength when she quickly adjusted her presentation after the client suddenly changed the meeting's agenda."

5. Repeat the process for every team member, ensuring that everyone's strengths are highlighted and appreciated.

6. After each member has been recognized, facilitate a discussion about how recognizing and appreciating others' strengths made them feel. Explore questions such as:

    o   How does it feel to hear your strengths recognized and appreciated by your peers?

    o   How can we integrate this appreciation into our daily work environment?

    o   How might recognizing and appreciating each other's strengths impact our team's dynamics?

Outcome: The Strengths Appreciation Exercise is a powerful tool for recognizing and validating each team member's unique strengths. It fosters a positive and supportive atmosphere within the team, ensuring that individuals feel valued and appreciated for their contributions.

It also boosts team morale and camaraderie, and is often a gateway to further discussions about how each member's strengths can be better utilized for team success. Regularly incorporating this exercise into your team routine can greatly reinforce a strengths-based culture, leading to increased engagement, satisfaction, and productivity.

5. Strengths Champions Activity

Objective: To deepen understanding and appreciation for each team member's unique strengths. This occurs through the "championing" of one person's strength by another, boosting personal growth and team cohesion.

Materials needed: The strengths assessment results from each team member, small slips of paper or sticky notes, and pens.

Procedure:

1. To start, ensure that each team member has taken a strengths assessment, such as Gallup's CliftonStrengths, StandOut, or VIA Character Strengths. Have them bring their top strengths to the activity.

2. Distribute slips of paper or sticky notes and pens to each participant, then ask each person to write their name and top five strengths on one slip.

3. Collect the slips and mix them up in a bowl or hat. Next, have each member draw one slip (making sure that they don't draw their own).

4. Once everyone has a slip, introduce the concept of "Strengths Champions." In this exercise, each person becomes the Strengths Champion for the individual whose slip they've drawn. Their task over the coming week will be to observe and note instances where that individual significantly uses their strengths. Encourage them to be as specific as possible in their observations. For instance, if you've drawn a slip for Megan, who has "Strategic" as one of her top strengths, you might note, "Megan used her strategic strength in the Monday team meeting when she proposed a new approach to tackle our project challenge."

5. At the end of the week, reconvene the group. Have each Strengths Champion share their observations about their person's strengths in action.

6. Encourage dialogue around the observations, with questions such as:

   o How did it feel to have your strengths observed and recognized?

   o Were there any surprises in the observations?

   o How can we continue to support each other in leveraging our strengths?

Outcome: The Strengths Champions Activity encourages team members to actively watch for and appreciate each other's strengths in action. This exercise cultivates a heightened awareness of each person's unique contributions, enhancing mutual respect and collaboration. It also reinforces a strengths-based mindset in the daily work environment, helping individuals to consistently recognize and capitalize on their strengths and the strengths of their colleagues. Over time, this exercise can contribute to a strong, supportive, and high-performing team culture.

6. Strengths Goal Setting Exercise

Objective: To enable team members to apply their unique strengths to their professional goals. This exercise allows individuals to reflect on how they can leverage their strengths to achieve their ambitions, fostering a proactive and empowered approach to professional growth.

Materials needed: The strengths assessment results from each team member, notepads, and pens.

Procedure:

1. Ensure that each team member has taken a strengths assessment and can identify their top strengths. They bring this information to the activity.

2. Start by explaining the purpose of the exercise—to identify how to utilize individual strengths to achieve personal and professional goals.

3. Hand out notepads and pens to each participant. Ask each person to list their top three strengths at the top of their notepad.

4. Next, have everyone write down at least one professional goal they're aiming to achieve in the next six months. For instance, if you're aiming to improve your project management skills, your goal might be to successfully lead a major project within this timeframe.

5. Once everyone has written down their goals, instruct them to reflect on how their top strengths can support them in achieving these goals. Ask them to write down specific actions they can take that align with their strengths to achieve their goals. For instance, if "Strategic" is one of your top strengths and your goal is to lead a major project, an action could be to create a comprehensive project plan that anticipates potential challenges and outlines alternative approaches.

6. After everyone completes this task, invite volunteers to share their goals, strengths, and action plans. Encourage open discussion and collaborative brainstorming around these shared insights.

7. Finally, facilitate a discussion, using questions such as:

o   How did it feel to connect your strengths with your professional goals?

o   What insights or surprises did you discover through this exercise?

o   How can we support each other in our goal pursuits?

Outcome: The Strengths Goal Setting Exercise helps to personalize the concept of strengths-based work, demonstrating how it directly applies to individual career growth. This activity empowers team members to harness their strengths for goal achievement, and it fosters a sense of self-efficacy and motivation. As everyone shares their goals and strategies, they can also identify ways to support each other and foster a supportive and collaborative environment. Ultimately, this exercise can help to create a proactive, strengths-based culture that supports individual and team success.

7. Strengths Swap Activity

Objective: To foster empathy and understanding within your team. It provides an opportunity for team members to experience another perspective—based on a different set of strengths. The exercise encourages active listening, mutual understanding, and appreciation for the diversity of strengths in the team.

Materials needed: The strengths assessment results from each team member, notepads, and pens.

Procedure:

1.   Ensure that each team member has a clear understanding of their top 3 to 5 strengths, as determined by their strengths assessment.

2. Explain the aim of the exercise: Team members swap strengths with a partner and explore how different strengths can be applied to various work situations.

3. Pair up team members, after which each pair will exchange their list of top 3 to 5 strengths.

4. Next, present a hypothetical work scenario to the group. This could be a complex problem that needs solving, a project that requires planning, or a challenging team dynamic that needs managing.

5. In their pairs, each team member takes a few minutes to consider how they'd approach this scenario using not their own but their partner's top strengths. They'll make notes of strategies and solutions they could employ using those particular strengths. For instance, if you're leveraging a partner's "Command" strength for a project-planning scenario, you might decide to take decisive action by clearly defining roles and expectations for the project team and leading the communication with stakeholders.

6. After this reflection time, partners share their strategies. This sharing provides an opportunity to learn how colleagues perceive each other's strengths, allowing for clarification and further understanding.

7. Once the pairs have shared, invite volunteers to share their insights with the larger group. This can lead to interesting discussions about different strengths and how they can be applied.

8. Conclude the session with a discussion about the experience. Use guiding questions, such as:

    o   How did it feel approaching a situation with a different set of strengths?

- o   What insights did you gain about your partner's strengths?

- o   How might this exercise impact future collaborations?

Outcome: The Strengths Swap Activity provides a unique perspective into how different strengths can approach the same situation in varying ways. It encourages empathy and appreciation for the diversity of strengths within the team, and it also sparks creative thinking by prompting team members to think outside their usual patterns and preferences. This increased understanding contributes to more effective collaboration, greater mutual respect, and an enhanced team dynamic.

8. Strengths and Weaknesses Audit

Objective: To develop an increased awareness and understanding of both the strengths and weaknesses within your team. This exercise not only promotes self-awareness but also encourages team members to consider how strengths compensate for weaknesses, leading to improved collaboration and productivity.

Materials needed: The strengths assessment results from each team member, notepads, and pens.

Procedure:

1.   Get everyone to identify their strengths and write them down on their notepad.

2.   Ask each member to reflect on and jot down what they perceive as their main weaknesses or areas needing improvement. Remind everyone that this is a supportive exercise; it's not meant for judgment but for growth and understanding.

3. Next, divide your team into pairs. In each pair, have team members share their strengths and weaknesses. This sharing process should be done with respect and kindness, and everyone should understand that vulnerability in this exercise leads to growth. For instance, a team member might share, "One of my strengths is 'Empathy,' which I think helps me to connect with team members and understand their perspectives. However, a weakness I've identified is time management. I sometimes get so caught up in supporting others that I lose track of my own tasks."

4. Once team members have shared, ask each pair to brainstorm ways they could use their strengths to mitigate their identified weaknesses. For example, the team member with "Empathy" as their strength might consider setting boundaries on task-times and using their empathetic nature to communicate these boundaries effectively to others.

5. Following the paired discussions, bring the team back together as a whole. Ask for volunteers to share what they've learned about their strengths and weaknesses, as well as how they plan to use their strengths to compensate for their weaknesses.

6. End the session by encouraging a team-wide discussion, with questions like:

   o How does understanding each other's strengths and weaknesses influence our team dynamic?

   o How can we better support each other in our areas of weakness?

   o How does this self-awareness influence our individual roles within the team?

Outcome: The Strengths and Weaknesses Audit helps to foster an environment of openness and understanding within your team.

By acknowledging both strengths and weaknesses, team members work more effectively by playing to their strengths and seeking help in areas of weakness. This exercise leads to greater mutual support, enhanced team cohesion, and improved individual and team performance.

9. Strengths-Based Feedback Exercise

Objective: To foster a culture of positive feedback within your team that's focused on individual strengths. It promotes appreciation, boosts morale, and helps to identify how individual strengths contribute to team success.

Materials needed: The strengths assessment results from each team member, paper, and pens.

Procedure:

1. Have each team member write down their top strengths from their assessment results.

2. Next, provide everyone with a piece of paper containing the names of their fellow team members. Beside each name, they should write down a specific instance when they saw that person utilize one of their top strengths effectively in the workplace. For example, a team member might write, "Luke used his 'Strategic Thinking' strength when he proposed a new approach to our project plan that addressed potential future obstacles."

3. Once everyone completes their list, gather your team in a circle. Starting with yourself, read out the strengths and instances you've written down for each person.

4. Continue around the circle, allowing each person to share their observations. Make sure everyone has an opportunity to speak and to hear positive feedback about their strengths.

5. Conclude the session by encouraging a discussion around the following questions:

    o   How does it feel to hear positive feedback about your strengths?

    o   How can we ensure that strengths-based feedback becomes a regular part of our team culture?

    o   How can we apply our strengths more effectively in the future?

Outcome: The Strengths-Based Feedback Exercise nurtures a positive and appreciative team culture, allowing members to understand how their individual strengths contribute to the team and how they're perceived by others. The process of giving and receiving positive feedback enhances team morale and cohesion. The activity encourages a strengths-focused approach to work, improving team productivity, engagement, and job satisfaction.

10. Strengths Challenge Activity

Objective: To practically apply strengths in everyday work situations. This enhances the understanding of individual strengths, and it fosters a team environment where these strengths are recognized and utilized regularly.

Materials needed: The strengths assessment results from each team member, note cards or a digital task management system, and markers or a digital tool for notetaking.

Procedure:

1. Ensure that everyone has their top five strengths from their assessment results handy.

2. Next, set up a challenge for your team that revolves around using their individual strengths in a specific, measurable way in their everyday work. The challenge could be a specific task or project, or a broader goal such as improving communication or team collaboration. For example, you might introduce a challenge like, "Use your top strength to improve the client proposal process in our team."

3. Each team member writes down or inputs into the digital tool how they plan to use their top strength to meet the challenge. They should be as specific as possible. For instance, if a team member's top strength is "Innovation," they might write, "I'll use my strength of 'Innovation' to devise a more engaging and visually dynamic proposal template."

4. Allow a set period (a week, a month, etc.) for team members to apply their strength to the challenge. Regular check-ins can be helpful to keep momentum going and provide support if needed.

5. At the end of the set period, gather the team and have each member share what they did and describe the impact it had on the challenge.

6. Facilitate a discussion with questions, such as:

    o   How did it feel to intentionally apply your strength to your work?

    o   What did you learn about your strength through this process?

    o   How can we continue to apply our strengths in our daily work?

Outcome: The Strengths Challenge Activity helps to embed a strengths-based culture into your team by encouraging the practical application of strengths in everyday work situations. It allows team members to gain a deeper understanding of their strengths and how they can be leveraged for greater success. It not only boosts team morale and productivity but also promotes a supportive environment where strengths are recognized and appreciated. It sets the tone for ongoing strengths-based development within the team.

About the Author

Dr. Christopher P. Meade holds a Ph.D. in Adult & Organizational Learning with a concentration in leadership. He also holds two master's degrees and a certificate in Disruptive Strategy from Harvard Business School. A former business school dean and acclaimed graduate instructor, Christopher has coached and trained more than 25,000 leaders and facilitated team training for numerous Fortune 500 organizations. Christopher speaks at leadership events and team training events throughout the United States. He is the author of multiple books on leadership and personal and professional development, including *Leadership Alive: Changing Leadership Practices in the Emerging 21st Century Culture; Leading Strategic Change, Innovation & Transformation: The 10 Elements of Successful Change Leadership; ETHIC: Leveraging the Human Factor in the Age of Artificial Intelligence and Accelerated Change; Trust Accelerators: Activating the Domino Effect That Accelerates Team Engagement, Innovation, and High-Performance; Trusted Servant Leadership: A New Kind of Leader for a New Kind of World; Servantology: The Periodic Elements of Servant Leadership; Team Accelerators: The Seven Force Multipliers of High-Performance Teams; DISC-Based Leadership: A Leader's Guide to Team Effectiveness; and Emotional Intelligence: Another Kind of Smart.*

> "I want to inspire leaders to be extraordinary. Everything I do is designed to catalyze growth in others and propel them toward a better version of themselves, so they can more meaningfully touch the lives of others in the work they do each day."
>
> — Christopher P. Meade, Ph.D.

www.ingramcontent.com/pod-product-compliance
Lightning Source LLC
Chambersburg PA
CBHW021551150726
47990CB00006B/2497